Money
&
Me

Financial Life Stories
of Successful People

Graham Rowan

First published 2019
Once Productions Limited,
20-22, Wenlock Road, London, England, N1 7GU

ISBN 978-0-9932449-4-0

Printed in Great Britain by
Biddles Books Limited, King's Lynn, Norfolk

Contents

Foreword
from Money Week editor John Stepek

You know what surprised me most when I first became a journalist? It's how willing people are to talk openly to a complete stranger, on any topic in the world that you care to question them on. It's all the more peculiar when you consider that journalists are by no means held in high esteem by society at large – indeed, we often find ourselves competing with politicians, bankers and estate agents for the title of "least-trusted" profession (worse still, we often win).

The reality, of course, is not that human beings want to talk to journalists – we just want to talk to anyone who'll listen. We're social animals. We each have our world view and our stories, and we want to share those stories with just about anyone who'll lend an ear and show an interest.

Graham Rowan, of course, isn't a journalist - he's a wealth coach and a financial educator. But he does excel at using this very human desire to talk about ourselves, to coax out valuable information on one of the most taboo topics in the world – money.

In this book, Graham delves into what he describes as the "financial life stories of successful people". I was flattered – if slightly bemused – to find myself among them. I'm more used to being interviewer than interviewee, but under Graham's friendly yet incisive questioning, atop a shiny skyscraper in Canary Wharf, I found myself revealing more about my background, and my childhood dreams of becoming a writer, than I ever thought I would.

I suspect the same is true for all of his interviewees. I know several of the people featured in this book, some of them – regular MoneyWeek contributors, Dominic Frisby and Tim Price in particular – very well indeed, and yet many of the stories they told Graham about their backgrounds and their motivations were revelations to me.

There are 17 interviews in this book in all, from which Graham has pulled a total of 51 "key lessons" – and I'm sure you'll find many more if you go through it with pen in hand, in the manner he suggests. And if that makes it sound like homework, I can assure you it's not. There are some great stories in here – from City stalwart Justin Urquhart Stewart's days as a shop steward, to entrepreneur Jonathan Jay's childhood business venture as a stage magician.

But are there any overarching lessons about success that can be drawn from these stories as a whole? At first glance, it doesn't look like it. Some of Graham's interviewees started out very early, with a clear goal in mind – James Sinclair, founder of The Partyman Group, is a born entrepreneur, building businesses and a significant income in his teens. Others – including me – came to their long-term careers via a more circuitous route.

Some were born into relative privilege, or even aristocracy, others hail from backgrounds where money was tight. Some have always been well organised, disciplined savers, such as the FT's Claer Barrett, whereas others – like serial entrepreneur and business coach Dan Bradbury – started out as born spenders. Some have built businesses. Others invest for a living (their own money and other people's). Others still are educators.

In short, there is no stand-out character trait or set of views or career path that these stories have in common. In fact, the only lesson that springs to mind is: "everyone is different". That may seem like a statement of the obvious and a not-terribly-helpful one at that.

But in fact, I think it's very liberating to realise that there is no single path to success. There is no "secret". Life is not about finding some hidden masterplan that leads to a satisfying career, or to a great deal of wealth, or both – it's about finding what works for you. So take this book, read the stories, find what resonates with you, and add it to your mental toolkit.

Oh, and enjoy it!

John Stepek

Executive editor, MoneyWeek
Author, The Sceptical Investor

Introduction

Congratulations on reading this far!

If you've so much as opened the cover of this book, I want to congratulate you.

The very act of holding this book in your hands puts you ahead of 95% of the population. I call them the Mediocre Majority. While you are scanning this page to see if **Money & Me** is worth reading further, they are busy entertaining themselves:

- Watching endless videos on Youtube.
- Playing repetitive computer games.
- Binge watching the latest TV drama series.
- Gambling away their spare cash online.
- Or watching pornography.

But you are clearly different. You have a curiosity to learn what others may know that you don't know. To study those who've already achieved some success and see what you can learn. And for that willingness to search out new information, I salute you.

You're going to enjoy this book. Why? Because the 17 financial life stories that you will read are as entertaining as they are educational. The vast majority of these people were not born to wealth and privilege. What they've got, they've earned. Their backgrounds are as diverse as their achievements, but they all demonstrate a willingness to share.

My role in this is a small one. My goal is to put myself in your place and ask the kind of questions you would ask if you were face to face with my guests. As you'll see, some can talk for England while others need a bit of cajoling. But each guest shares some nuggets about how they've climbed the greasy pole to success in their field. Most of the secrets they share can be applied in your life with only the smallest tweaks to fit your unique circumstances.

How To Use This Book

How can you get the most from this book? Do what I do, much to the annoyance of my wife who regards books as sacred tomes to be kept pristine for posterity. To me, a book is a learning tool from which I want to extract the 5% that will make the biggest difference in my life. So I read with a brightly coloured marker pen in hand, highlighting the lines that tell me something new. Then I re-read it with a focus on the highlighted sections. If they still strike me as valuable, I write them into a Word document from which I formulate an action plan.

Yes, that's a lot of work. But your life will only change if you take action on the things you've learned. Study the 17 guests and you'll find another commonality. They're not afraid of putting in the hard yards to achieve mastery in their field. So many people are looking for the Easy Button. You can marry it, divorce it or inherit it. Otherwise, wealth and success tend to be hard task masters who only smile on the deserving.

The trick is to avoid the mistakes that others have made and accelerate your own journey to success. What better way of doing that than absorbing the success secrets of 17 outstanding achievers, one short chapter at a time?

To give the book a bit of structure, I've carved the 17 interviews up into five sections – Fund Managers, Entrepreneurs, Writers, Coaches and Celebrities. Each chapter starts with a profile of the guest, followed by the transcript of the studio interview we filmed for the first series of *Money & Me* that aired on Sky TV in 2018 and 2019. All I've done is eliminate the *ums* and *ahs* and the *likes* and *you knows* to improve readability.

There's no law that says you must read the book in the order it appears – if Wimbledon commentator John Inverdale is of most interest, why not start there? If you're a serious stock market investor you've probably heard of Justin Urquhart Stewart – he is a raconteur *par excellence* so I know you'll relish his interview. I found Claer Barrett, Financial Journalist of the Year and editor of the FT Money section of the Weekend Financial Times, to be one of the most enjoyable discussions in the series. If you remember the first series of The Apprentice or you're a fan of LBC and Talk Radio, James Max will need no introduction. It turns out he is a good friend of both Claer and Justin, and you'll love his periodic FT articles on Rich People's Problems.

Since recording the interview with art expert Aidan Meller, he has gone on to world-wide fame as the creator of the world's first robotic artist, Ai-Da. In the week of her first exhibition in Oxford in June 2019 she appeared in 857 TV and radio programmes, newspapers and websites across the globe. Over £1.6 million of her work was sold ahead of the exhibition and more invitations are arriving daily as her fame spreads.

If business is your thing, there's a fascinating mix of entrepreneurs to learn from including Luke Lang, co-founder of the world's biggest equity crowdfunding platform, the aristocratic Marquess of Bristol who has established a property focused platform and Jonathan Jay who has bought and sold more than 25 businesses and now teaches others to do the same. James Sinclair started life as a children's entertainer and now runs a £10 million leisure and childcare business as well as finding time to write a book that is appropriately entitled 'Millionaire Clown'.

Lord Stanley Fink could arguably be placed in two of our groupings, as he initially became known as the 'Godfather of Hedge Funds' for his work with Man Group, before focusing on becoming a serial entrepreneur and philanthropist. You will also learn from Dan Bradbury, a business coach who enables you to scale your enterprise by putting in systems and processes that take you out of the equation. (*Note to self – maybe I need Dan's help*).

One of the must-read publications for any serious UK investor is Money Week, and we've mined that seam deeply to include Executive Editor John Stepek, gold and cryptos expert Dominic Frisby and value investing guru *cum* fund manager Tim Price. Dominic and Tim both produce hugely entertaining blogs and videos that you should seek out if you don't already know them.

There's also quite a strong property investment theme in the book, with Australia's Nicole Bremner sharing her story of moving from stay-at-home mum to sitting astride a £100 million property empire. John Howard took over the family estate agency business in his late teens and trebled it by his early twenties. That was just the start of an illustrious career as a property developer. Both are now busy coaching others in how to succeed in property investing, whereas Siam Kidd coaches in a very different sector. He is focused on the more volatile world of trading the crypto markets, quickly disabusing those who come to him with a 'get rich quick' mentality. First, you have to treat it like a business, not a hobby. Then, you have to allow three to five years to develop the deep skills needed to succeed. Needless to say, many with the attention span of a gnat fall by the wayside…

17 people. 17 financial life stories. If you only find one 'writer downer' in each chapter, that's seventeen reasons why you should turn the page. Good news – I've done that for you by extracting 3 Key Lessons from each interview that you can find at the end of each chapter. If you're too busy to read the chapters, turn to the back to see all 51 lessons laid out ready to implement. I can do no more! The rest is up to you.

Enjoy the book. Enjoy the journey.

Graham

Cap D'Antibes, France, August 17th 2019

Section 1

The Fund Managers

Justin Urquhart Stewart

Tim Price

Lord Stanley Fink

Justin Urquhart Stewart

Justin Urquhart Stewart
Using Red Braces To Make Finance Fun

In the staid world of financial services, Justin Urquhart Stewart is a breath of fresh air. He has a delightfully chequered background that includes being a shop steward on Southampton docks and being shot while working for Barclays Bank in Uganda.

Having been a prime mover in the Big Bang that revolutionised the City, Justin was also quick to realise the media potential as investing began to go mainstream in the 1980s. He became a fixture on our TV screens on any and all financial programmes, his red bow tie and braces creating an instant personal brand.

He really found his niche at the turn of the millennium when he and fellow ex Barclays man Tom Sheridan set up 7 Investment Management. Implementing his strategy of massive diversification and low management charges, 7IM has mushroomed into a major fund management corporation with over 300 staff and more than £14 billion under management.

Justin can be seen driving round West London in his pristine Morris Minor Traveller, that is when he's not burning up the highway rather more quickly on one of his motorbikes.

In this interview he gives us a whistle stop tour through his career before homing in on my own mission – the desperate need for financial education for people of all ages.

In this chapter my guest is possibly Britain's best known financial pundit and also the founder of one of our most successful investment management companies, Justin Urquhart Stewart. Justin welcome to Money & Me.

Thank you very much; it's nice to be here.

Now obviously today you're known as a fine upstanding figure in the financial community, but at the risk of shocking the British public, I have to say that back in the playground, when you were 7 years old, I hear you were a bit of a dealer?

How to get yourself into serious trouble! My first efforts at actually trying to make some money and getting thoroughly punished for it. In those days Mars Bars were really expensive, they were a tradable item, and what I had worked out was if I had got my father's razor blade, and of course in those days, they were terribly big blades, and I chopped it up into seven pieces, I could sell off six pieces and make some profit and then buy another Mars Bar and keep the last bit for myself. Then the teacher stopped me and I got hauled off and got thoroughly whacked for it, not for actually carrying out early forms of capitalism, but for having a dangerous instrument in the form of a razor blade!

Oh my goodness -obviously a very, very dangerous background. But of course you were brought up in a military family I believe? What was that environment like and was the subject of money ever brought up in the family?

Money was never ever talked about in the slightest, mainly because they hadn't got a clue about it! I'm the odd one out, all of them have joined the army for generations back. Life with my mother was a bit confusing because she went through three husbands, one of whom purported to be my father, but the detail is hazy. However she was always rather keen and said, 'what are you going to do with your life?' And I said 'actually I want to have my own business'. And she looked down her rather long nose at me and said 'oh my God you want to go into trade, do you realise we have a separate door for that?'

And that in many ways summed up the British attitude in those days, we weren't entrepreneurial, you either worked for the State or you worked for the Services and the Government, or you were a professional or you worked for a large corporation. Did you have your own business? No of course you didn't. So the idea of actually having your own business was disregarded, it was 'oh go and get a proper job'. And eventually I was told to go off and be a lawyer, which was just dreadful.

Indeed, well we have one thing in common - I studied law at university, but at least I had the decency to drop out. You actually completed the course and trained as a Barrister, so how did you avoid this fate worse than death of being a lawyer?

By realising that actually *being* a Barrister was incredibly dull. My Pupil Master, the person who trains you as you're doing these sort of things, said 'Justin, do you realise there's more money in crime than defending it?' So, at that moment, I thought financial services - now there's a crime! So actually you could earn some money, but also you could make a bit of a difference. As a Barrister you're at the end of the line, I had to make sure you had a bad problem, the worse your problem the happier I'd be. That's not a good place to be in.

No, indeed.

So what you want to do is actually create something, build something, do something which makes a difference.

We're getting ahead of ourselves here because despite your early attempt at entrepreneurship, when you actually got to university to study law you did start to get into some trouble with debt I believe?

Yes I was useless, absolutely useless. Building up debt with the joy of a credit card. What was that for? Well just money to spend, I didn't realise you actually spent up to the limit and now you can't pay it down. I had no knowledge at all and I was a spoiled brat. Of course in those days you didn't have student debt, I was able to achieve that on my own, I didn't need the government to help me into debt! But no, it was frankly pathetic and it really does reflect what's happened in Britain - we don't teach people financial management and how to look after themselves. We teach people economics, like we need another economist.

Exactly, so how did you overcome this debt that you left university with?

It just took a very long time to try and sort it all out. I realised of course, once you got yourself into it, this is dumb, this is stupid, how would you actually dig yourself out of it? You just have to learn it by pain and by realising you have to go out and work. And I ended up on Southampton Docks. I think I'm the only shop steward in the London Stock Exchange...

Shop steward! You!

Yes, Union of Constructional Allied Technical Trades. I was not called Justin because that would not go down terribly well, not Urquhart Stewart either, so I'm actually a member known as John Stewart and I was shop steward for UCATT on Southampton Docks.

A proud boast.

I got very well paid for it, it helped pay off the credit card debt so it was good.

Excellent. So you decide that being a Barrister is not for you, how do you make this leap into financial services, was there some kind of road to Damascus moment?

Well it was actually more desperation and what can you do? One of the things I did get involved in was trade, actually understanding trade, how traded widgets go from one place to another and around the world. And, of course, in the military that again is how things get passed round the world. So I joined an old fashioned British trading bank, Barclays DCO, Dominion, Colonial and Overseas. You virtually had a white hat to go with the name.

And I remember when they said we're going to send you off for some proper training and I thought that's jolly good. He had this huge book of all the places in the world that Barclays DCO existed and it went from Anguilla right the way through to Zambia. I remember this Director going through the entire list of countries, I thought this is getting worse and worse and worse, till eventually we got to virtually the end of it and I thought 'well I'm going to end up going to Zaire'. And he said 'Uganda; we need more people in Uganda', I said 'but there's a war on there', he said 'exactly, that's why we need more people there!'.

Excellent.

There's a start.

I think you'd call that a hospital pass. So how was life in the Uganda branch of Barclays Bank?

Somewhat limited on the basis I had a slight technical hitch - there was a coup after a few months and I found myself in hospital (*Justin's inherited military sangfroid forbids him from mentioning that the 'technical hitch' was getting shot – GR*). But any way that was all fine and dandy. But it taught you about proper trade finance, how do you get goods exported from Britain, from elsewhere around the world, properly financed, constructed and actually then making sure that they're properly embedded in that country and vice versa as well. Good old-fashioned trading and that was the bit that I learned there.

So Justin, after your entry into the banking world, it wasn't that long before you got involved in one of the biggest changes in our Stock Market's history, the Big Bang.

Yeah, well that came about, because I'd been working out in Singapore and first we had Baby Bang as part of the build up and development of all this. This was going to be the real reorganisation of the City, because the City was an old-fashioned cartel of how things used to work (not very efficiently), then a tendency to re-write history. Big Bang was going to inject huge amounts of mostly American money coming into the old world of broking. So I came back to help with that as part of Barclays, they built something called BZW, which was Barclays de Zoete Wedd, and basically they got de Zoete & Bevan that are a broking firm, Wedd Durlacher are a market making jobbing firm and welded it together with Barclays Merchant Bank, which no one had heard of even in Barclays. And that created this coordinated group, which was going to be able to provide services to everybody, and of course it turned out to be a complete mess.

Oh dear.

It was a lovely concept but no one had really thought it through and millions was wasted on this. But it taught me to understand how the broking operations, the underlying systems, were working badly. And from that we set up a business called Broker Services, which white labelled lots of other stockbrokers, people like Salomon's, to operate in the City and we could actually do the trading and the settlement for them. That organisation ended up being the UK's largest stockbroker.

And is that when you started doing your market updates that turned into this glittering media career?

It just so happened that BZW was being reorganised by Barclays again and they had a camera on their trading floor. So I got my messenger, I gave him a letter of authority to go in there and I said look, if there's any chance of actually getting the camera out let me know, if anyone challenges you just keep quiet. He phones up an hour later and says 'Justin, I've got a problem' and I said 'what's that?' 'It's stuck to the wall', I said 'oh I'm sorry, forget it, don't worry about it', he said 'no, no I'm just going to be a bit longer', I said 'no Peter, no leave it'. An hour later he turns up with a wall with a camera attached to it. So therefore we ended up with this camera and needed BT to get it connected. They moved at their typical speed, so about six months later we got it working. We phoned up Bloomberg, who were just starting

Bloomberg television and all those sort of things, and said 'do you want a market report?' and off it went from there.

Wow and did you have the red accoutrements from day one or is that something that came in a bit later?

I was mostly red because my father had red braces and things like that but I had other ones as well, but the red seemed to stick, it was a bit corny but now I'm stuck with them and all my trousers now have red braces, so at least I don't have to choose in the morning.

So you're now up and running, you've got the Broker Services business and you're regularly in the media. Let's talk about your own investment portfolio - you've obviously been investing in the Stock Market and you've also invested in property, what would you say has been your best investment personally Justin?

It's a corny line to say, but my answer is investing in yourself because actually that's where most of the positive things have come from. Yes trying things, so people say have a go at property and have a go at this, but I found I wasn't that expert in it. What I did find was I did understand the investment world and how that was operating and how that could change.

And we were based in Glasgow as well as London because Glasgow of course had its own Stock Exchange. In those days there were seven regional Stock Exchanges - they should have them still but never mind. And what was interesting there, we developed what became AIM. A group of us wanted to do a smaller companies market because what's the purpose of the Stock Exchange? Not to buy and sell shares, it's to raise capital in the most cost efficient and effective manner possible and there wasn't really a smaller companies market doing it properly.

So AIM was eventually taken over by the Stock Exchange. Unfortunately, it's not what it should be, but nonetheless it gave us the opportunity to understand how that should develop and how proud investors could get involved with privatisations and de-mutualisations - that world of popular share ownership which has sadly died away now. But it got people to the idea of understanding more about investing and I realised that this is at least part of the education we can pass on to people to give them a better idea.

Okay and you touched there on I think what is becoming a bigger and bigger issue now, which is that fewer companies are going on the public stock markets and the choice for the investor is actually diminishing.

It has been diminishing and the days when people were having lots of initial public offerings (IPOS), that is new share issues, so 'join in with this and have a punt on these', it doesn't really happen very much. Now I think that will come back again because there's going to be a restructuring of this over the next few years, but what it has meant is that people have had to learn other ways of investing, through property, through other assets, through funds and things like that. But fundamentally they are in a weak position because they weren't taught about the costs, the charges, what returns they had to achieve, and of course all the rule changes around pensions, bless the politicians. The good news is we're all living longer; the bad news is we're all living longer but no one's told you how to afford it. That's what we have to be able to try and teach people to do.

Absolutely - I think one of the biggest challenges that we both see is that people, even successful people, seem to be almost financially illiterate. What's been your experience of it and what can be done to improve this?

It is astonishing isn't it and everyone will say well of course the schoolchildren don't understand, well of course no they don't because we don't teach it, it's not in the curriculum. Okay people are starting to make an effort towards it but still it's tiny. But that's not necessarily the issue; adults running their businesses, they're perfect at running their businesses, you then look at their finances, its awful! What have you done about your pension, what have you done for your family, what about your parents' position or grandparents or of course great grandparents? People say 'I'm making widgets, I can make money at widgets, I know about that. Well, what about money? 'Oh, I don't do that. I go to my accountant'. Well they do the audit and that's about all they do. Their lawyer? They won't get much out of that. Bank? Oh I don't want to go near the banks. A lot of the IFAs, I'm not too sure I'm necessarily going to go there. Stockbrokers, I wouldn't even know what they look like. And so I'll make widgets instead. And so they just bury their heads in the sand.

The good news is in Britain we are now setting up more businesses than ever before; we have become so much more entrepreneurial than we were in my era. But now the problem is, it's all very well being entrepreneurial, now teach them to make sure they've got their finances right. You wouldn't set up a business in this country without a proper business plan, so why don't you look at your personal finances and have a plan? There's a corny line, if you're planning to invest don't. There you are that's me out of business. Invest in planning, get the plan right and everything else sort of fits into place. Your investments don't have to be hugely exciting and dangerous, they just have to be pretty run of the mill, steady stuff because it's time in the market that counts, not timing the market. Just let it grow over time but get the plan right first and most people will be where they need to be.

I know you have a schedule that makes me look positively slothful but you manage to take time out every few weeks to go and speak to kids about this - what are the kind of messages you're telling children about financial planning?

Just very straightforward stuff, not necessarily in terms of this is a stock and share and this, that and the other, but sitting there saying right okay, over the period of your life your parents are living now, that's very nice, they're going to be living another 20-30 years, how much money are they going to need, I wonder how much money you're going to need? And one of the things I've found, is actually some of our clients write software games and they actually wrote things like Donkey Kong, which I know is a bit out of date now, but Donkey Kong made things relatively simple and straight forward. Apply those software games to financial services and now you're teaching people about things like this in, dare I say, an entertaining or at least an engaging way. About things like pensions and how much money they need to retire on. Not so much to tell you what the answer is, but teaching people what the problem is so at least they can ask an intelligent question. How do I fix this problem rather than perhaps falling into the hands of some greasy salesman saying here's another product, you need another one of these funds or pensions or something like that and you just desperately cross your fingers and hope its going to work. That's rubbish; we must get people with a level of knowledge and intelligence to make the right decisions.

Yes indeed, but we're not really helped in this by the politicians, who seem to treat things like pensions as political footballs and they change the rules all the time and every year it seems like there's some kind of new regulation, but there's never anything that says now we're going to insist on a certain level of financial education so you can make more informed decisions.

That's the issue, if people had better understanding to start with, then you wouldn't need to have the regulation to stop the horrors occurring in the first place. So they've got the things the wrong way round, but it's better politics that way, I can make noises about how we need more regulation for this, that and the other. Better to teach people an understanding of how they could feed themselves. It's the old fishing rod thing isn't it – trying to regulate fish rather than teach people how to catch them - that's ridiculous.

I totally agree. So you've got your own daughter now, what have you taught her about money and at what age did you start the process of educating her about money?

I've taught her all I know and the result is useless, nothing at all! Yes she understands it, does she practice what I preach, no not in the slightest. But having said that, yes she does sort of understand it and she now understands about living on a budget and those sort of things, but in terms of really understanding proper financial planning, it's a case of 'oh, get somebody else to do that'. It's a shame, but still, I made a desperate effort!

I think the other side of this matter for me is that life is becoming so much more complicated and most financial planners think we're still living in the 1950s, where you've got mum, dad and 2.4 kids. The reality now is both are divorced with kids from a first relationship, then they have kids of their own.

Welcome to the great British dysfunctional family.

Exactly.

You know there's your second hand husband and wife, there are various selections of children, have the blood test done to check they're yours and a black Labrador, that might be yours too. Then you've got of course your parents, nice they're living longer, unfortunately also her parents. Grandparents - there are millions of them cluttering up golf courses around the countryside and then moving to Worthing. Great grandparents - we'd forgotten about them or maybe they've forgotten where they are. So you've got five generations of people.

Now if you just coordinated the finances for them, produce a family balance sheet, you suddenly realise your family is worth quite a lot, the assets are there, you avoid duplication, cut out the costs and then in terms of the amount of debt you've got in terms of the next generation having mortgages and things, the family can organise that far better and reduce the cost. If we could start having Family Offices for the British middle class we can start controlling what's happening here and we're not so dependent upon the politicians and it will give us the one word that runs any economy that we need to have which you'll never get off the politicians, 'confidence'.

Absolutely. Amen to that.

Confidence that, irrespective of what's going to happen over the elements of politics, Europe and the US Presidents and things like that, at least my family is going to be okay.

But ultimately that comes down to this rather emotional decision to take personal financial control doesn't it?

Yes.

And my challenge is, even with successful people, how do you get to that? For me it was when my Wealth Managers lost me £151,000, I thought 'well I can't do any worse than that'. Have you got any suggestions on how we can get people to just take this whole issue a bit more seriously?

If we can make it engaging for people, you can't make it entertaining, but make it interesting so that people can sit there and say if you do this, this happens, and actually you can see over a while how your wealth starts to grow. And you have an idea, this is the target we've got to get to, and you say actually you're okay, you're heading that way.

Because most of us don't really think about it too far and you then look back and see what's happened to the past 30 years, I've missed out, I should have done something. If you could just give yourself the targets of what the family needs to be able to achieve in terms of those asset values, that's going to give you the confidence. You don't know what's going to happen in the future, but what you've done has made sure that most of the family is going to be okay.

And I've put that into my family now, so that with my sister, her children, we've made sure the education costs are covered, the greater family can pay for that, then people will pay back into it as well, the family will start, not buying the house, but at least start the mortgage, get that going. So giving people the starters but understanding the responsibilities they've got to go with it as well. That I think is the way we start to try to go about it.

Because there's going to be this enormous transfer of wealth between the generations isn't there and I worry about whether say the Millennials are ready to be stewards of that family wealth.

Absolutely and it's a one off issue because over the next few decades, including me and you, we disappear and so actually we've got to be able to do this over the next few years and make sure the Millennials do realise that yes, we were the ones who benefited from the property boom, they've got the property bust, but if they can take all those issues in terms of those assets coming through to them and manage those properly over time, they're going to be okay.

Well there's a lot of education and planning still to do.

Yes!

Now we've talked a little bit about how you give back in terms of your time with schools, but you're also getting involved in a new initiative called Investors in Community, what's that all about?

This is a whole new idea whereby companies increasingly have to have a form of social responsibility. And there's going to be more of that, what are you doing to make sure, as a company, you're giving back? Because I was always taught in terms of business school things, you've got various groups you have to look after. Your, that awful word, stakeholders, which are your employees and shareholders. But also your customers and the people you actually work with, but also society as a whole.

If you upset any one of those groups you'll get heartily kicked, the banks managed to upset all of them and quite rightly got a hearty kicking.

So companies are increasingly going have to start saying what they are doing. Now look inside the companies, a lot of those people are doing a lot of good charitable stuff, often off their own back, they're putting money in, so why don't companies have a means of actually measuring this? And those that are participating earn community credits and those community credits can be cashed in for cups of coffee and other bits and pieces, but they can measure how much and they're getting some recognition for what they're doing. Maybe not the company for what they're participating in, but what their employees are doing can be measured, so they can turn around to their shareholders and say this is what we're doing.

So it helps companies actually make sure that they're behaving the right way and to measure it. It allows the employees to participate and get some recognition for it and measure it and it will be there on their CV, when they go for their next job, what have you done to try and help, well actually it's here and I can translate it into those community credits. That's what we can try and do.

So it's not patronising, it's actually allowing people to get recognition and companies to start taking control of this.

Okay, so I spoke recently at an event called Wealth & Society, which was all about philanthropy and what they said was the big problem was that its all too fragmented and we need to try and bring all this energy and effort together to tackle the big issues, is that one of the things you hope to achieve?

Well yes because what it can do is allow people then to control where they're doing their charitable giving, it will also cut out some of the cost for it as well. With all those charitable givings, suddenly you find 5% disappears in costs, actually no, we don't have to do the 5%, so you can reduce that cost. We can also corral that giving into not just charities, but into local projects, sometimes larger ones that companies themselves want to get involved in as well as employees this allows it to happen and for those involved to then get some recognition for it. If you can do that, reduce the cost and increase the proportion we're giving back into society, then I think that will be very helpful.

Fantastic! Well I've got lots more I'd love to talk to you about but sadly we've run out of time. So Justin Urquhart Stewart thank you very much.

A pleasure, thanks a lot.

Three Key Lessons
From Justin Urquhart Stewart

1. **Invest in your education** – this can include working a job to get the knowledge you need to launch a business. The more you learn, the more successful you will be in your chosen field.

2. **Personal branding** – Justin's red bow tie, pocket square and braces are as much a part of his success as the words he says in his media appearances. You need to stand out from the crowd more than ever, so pay attention to creating your own brand and be consistent with it as you grow your following

3. **Think of your extended family as a company** and form a Family Office to run everyone's financial affairs. If you can overcome unwillingness to share information, the benefits of scale can be significant. This is especially true for today's complex family structures with multiple generations, multiple marriages with children from each and with the biggest wealth transfer in human history about to go down.

Tim Price

Tim Price
The Writer Who Walks His Own Talk

Tim Price is one of my favourite people in the investing world. Why? Because he has deep rooted convictions about investing that he sticks too regardless of changing trends or fads, and because he articulates his beliefs in such an entertaining way.

Whether it's his columns in Money Week, his blog at The Price of Everything or in his book Investing Through the Looking Glass: A Rational Guide to Irrational Markets, Tim turns potentially dry topics into literary works of art. Go read them and see what I mean.

Most financial journalists can snipe and moan from the sidelines with impunity – Tim has to come into the office every day and make real investment decisions about what to do with real people's money. They've given him their funds to manage mainly because they buy into what he writes about, so he really does have to take his own medicine and live or die by the results.

In this interview Tim expands on his concept of value investing and gives some pointers about how to survive in an era of Brexit and Corbyn.

My guest in this chapter is perhaps best known as a writer in Money Week Magazine, but his day job has been as a Wealth Manager for some time now until about three years ago when he gave up his cushy job in the city and launched his own investment fund to implement the value investing strategy that he believes in. His name is Tim Price. Tim welcome to Money & Me.

Thanks very much for having me.

Now before we talk about investing and what you're doing today, let me put you on the psychiatrist's couch and take you back to your childhood. Tell me a little bit about the sort of family environment you grew up in and whether things like money were ever discussed or mentioned?

Funnily enough I don't think money was really a particularly big issue despite the fact that both my parents worked in finance; my dad worked in insurance, my mum was a bookkeeper, so there is a sort of a back-story there of finance, but it wasn't anything that particularly interested me. So I read English at university and fully intended to get into journalism as a profession. I had the misfortune to graduate in 1991, which if you remember was quite a bad recession year. So, by a kind of historical fluke, I ended up in the City instead, I ended up as a Bond Salesman.

I've kept up writing since because I enjoy writing, but my day job has been much more capital markets-related. So frankly I've managed to have my cake and eat it because I get to have a bit of both worlds.

Right, so there was no grand plan to get into finance, you thought you wanted to be a writer but then there just weren't the openings?

Yeah I had a bit of experience working in journalism, I had a great two summers working at magazine called Literary Review, who's Editor you might remember, Auberon Waugh, a very entertaining very lovely guy. I got some internships, I think the Daily Express was one; they had an ill-fated magazine called DX Magazine. So I got a bit of experience but that experience frankly did not super encourage me to stay in journalism. So, when there weren't really any opportunities for me to grasp in the early 90s, I wasn't too fussed by that.

Interesting because I suppose a lot of people these days might aspire to go and work in the City and finance and for you it was almost like a fallback.

That's exactly what it was. It was a bit like John Major running away from the circus to become an accountant.

Right, I guess he did alright in the end.

He did okay.

So you start working now in the finance sector as a bond salesman, what was your own attitude towards personal investing at that point?

I guess I've always been inclined to be a saver rather than a spender. It's a Dickens' quote, I forget the character but he says if your outgoings are x and your income is a little bit higher than x that's fine, but if it's the other way round you're in trouble. So as long as you can keep the ship steady everything's fine. Suffice to say as soon as I was able to get rid of my liabilities like the mortgage then that was the first thing that was going to go. So I don't like being indebted, I don't like being leveraged in that respect. And I think in an investment context, leverage is maybe one of the worst things that can happen because it tends to be the life or death event for a lot of managers.

So you wouldn't make much of a politician if you're not good at debt then would you?

No, I mean to answer a sort of semi-serious question seriously, the first thing I would do if I had any political influence would be to insist that politicians have to adopt a balanced budget strategy. Because the way that we currently have endless expenditure on nonsense is ultimately the way that madness lies, so at some point someone is going to have to steady the ship.

The book that you wrote is called Investing Through the Looking Glass: A Rational Guide to Irrational Markets - what was the thinking behind the book? The title obviously gives quite a bit away but what was the thinking behind it and how can we become rational about these irrational markets?

It's a good question. Writing a book about my experience in capital markets and the recent history of central banking and investment markets *per se* was a very cathartic exercise - I managed to exorcise a few private demons that I've experienced over the last 25 years. I think the average investor probably is unaware of just the kind of monetary insanity that we've been living through for not just the last ten years, though it's been extreme since 2008 and the financial crisis, but actually this insanity ultimately goes back to the early 1970s. Up to then we had a monetary system where currencies were backed by gold and then at one fell swoop President Nixon, I think in 1971, basically just took the dollar off gold. From that moment on we've had a currency system globally that's not backed by anything. The logical outcome of that is that you have a world that is now drowning in debt, which is exactly where we are today.

And what's the prognosis from here because I've been hearing and agreeing with that argument for many years now and to be honest, expecting some kind of Armageddon event and so far it hasn't happened. So are we fooling ourselves that it never will or is the world able to just continue piling up debt forever?

I think Grant Williams, who is a great writer and a very affable guy, said *'hasn't isn't the same as won't'*. So just because we've been living with this, what I would call monetary insanity for decades now, doesn't mean that there won't come the day of resolution or some way of dealing with the predicament.

But another way of looking at it I guess would be, you know the Soviet Union was born in the chaos of the Revolution in 1917, and pretty much every year consistently from that point on, intelligent, well informed outside observers would say this is just a house of cards, its going to collapse. The Berlin War didn't fall until 1989, that's how long a dysfunctional system can last; it can outlive all of us.

Right okay, so that means we have to take our own investment decisions during and within that dysfunctional system. You've had a few decades now to watch this unfolding and how has that influenced your own approach to investing for yourself and for your clients?

Okay, good question. I like to write but I also like to read a lot. I'm not a trained economist - I read English not economics - so I fill in the gaps from reading of things called books, which are apparently coming back into fashion.

Wow, radical.

And the one that really made an impact was a book called *'Against the Gods'* by Peter Bernstein that I came across in the late 1990s. Within that book there is a quote from a guy called Daniel Bernoulli, so it's a slightly extended thing but apologies for that. Daniel Bernoulli was a Renaissance man who lived a few hundred years ago, a Swiss-Italian mathematician and he said the following which is within *'Against the Gods: The History of Risk'* and I'd recommend it to anybody. Bernoulli said, if you're managing money for wealthy people 'the practical utility of any gain in portfolio value inversely relates to the size of the portfolio'. Or in plainer English, if you're managing money for wealthy people just don't lose it, they've already got their money, they don't need super normal returns, but what they do want is capital preservation.

And in 1998/99 when I came across that book it was like a blinding flash of the obvious that what the average investor probably wants, and certainly what the average wealthy investor probably wants, is basically an absolute return on their portfolio, they want capital preservation and inflation protection. No matter what they do, that's probably the outcome they'd most desire.

I'd certainly agree with that for those who have already accumulated their wealth.

I think that is also relevant for anybody. I think there's a presumption that people who aren't that wealthy can afford to take a bit more risk but I think people are naturally risk averse.

I think they are, I suppose the question is in an era of 4,000 year low interest rates, volatile stock markets and so on, somebody who is trying to accumulate wealth is probably trying to find some way of getting above market returns at least with part of their portfolio, so how do we suggest they go about that as opposed to the person whose got lots of capital they just want to conserve?

Well the way I'd square this circle is to say, at the end of the day I'm not convinced that index relative or market relative investing is appropriate for any investor. I don't think it's appropriate for the private investor in the same way that I'd say absolute return, i.e. cash plus or inflation plus as an objective makes sense because you can't take relative returns to the bank. And I think that a growing number of investors out there are getting increasingly disenchanted at the fund management industry or a fund manager saying 'well last year the market lost 20, we only lost 15 so we outperformed by 5', it's a nonsense argument.

Okay but I think you've touched there on what's probably the biggest trends we're seeing at the moment which is people piling into these ETF tracker funds and I guess the problem with that is, if the whole market is going down, you're going down with it. So are you saying you're more of a stock picker and an active fund manager?

I think I've probably been what I would describe as a value investor since I started work and I think, whether it's value or whether it's growth, it's probably something you're born with, it's something you're naturally drawn to. So if someone wanted to know what I call value investing is all about I'd say it's trying to buy dollar bills for 40 cents, its trying to identify high quality businesses – it's typically valued through Stock Market listed companies – high quality businesses run by principled shareholder friendly management where the shares of those businesses for whatever reason, are available at a big discount to what those companies are really worth. So it's getting something cheap that's still good.

The all-time great value investor was Benjamin Graham who literally wrote the book, 'The Intelligent Investor' all about value investing and he is also the guy that taught Warren Buffet, so he doesn't really need any further introduction than that. But the thing that Ben Graham identified was this concept of 'margin of safety'. If you're a value investor, it doesn't matter what the market is doing, if you're a value investor and what you own gets cheaper you typically buy more of it because it was cheap to begin with. So if its cheaper and high quality you're just getting it at a bigger and bigger discount. The really amazing thing, the really mystifying thing about the investment markets for me and I dare say for you, is that how we behave is much more important than the figures or the data – it's so much a behavioural issue. And there's a guy in the States who said the Stock Market is like a shop where things go on sale and everyone rushes out of the shop!

I hear you Tim but my guess is, when you talk about buying a well managed company at a low price, I would have thought when you apply your filter you come up with a fairly short list in today's markets?

That's a fair point. Well lets roll the clock back, we've had ten years of extraordinary monetary accommodation from central banks and what that means is we've had quantitative easing (QE) plus zero interest rate policies (ZIRP) and, as you said earlier, we've had interest rates that have been at 4,000/5,000 year lows. Now that's a huge deal because those interest rates are now finally starting to go up and that has massive implications, particularly for bond holders.

So it's absolutely true that a lot of stuff is over priced, that bargains are not that thick on the ground. That said, he died a few years ago, but a great Canadian value investor, Peter Cundill, said 'there's always something to do'. Now those bargains may not be in the UK, I'd argue that the UK market is probably fairly priced but it's not massively cheap and there's clearly an ongoing political back-story. But if the UK isn't delivering the goods then we'll go somewhere that is. And where we're finding the, if you like, diamonds in the rough is in Asia - markets like Japan and Vietnam.

So you're both doing that on behalf of investors but also within your fund. If you look at the concept of a value fund, how would the contents of that differ from perhaps most of the investment funds that people would be familiar with out there?

Our fund is a little bit odd in that we own both specialist third party managed funds and also individual stocks. So at the level of individual stocks we can clearly say what are we looking for - we're looking for clearly great businesses, good managers, obviously cheap prices. To put some flesh on the bone in what cheap prices means, cheap valuations, if it's a price to earnings ratio, we want it to be ideally less than 15 times. If it's priced at book for example, priced to inherent value, we want to buy shares on a price to book of less than one and a half, ideally less than one times. Those are the kind of metrics that we're looking at.

But in terms of foreign markets, because we want to have the biggest opportunity set possible, we don't just want to fall victim to home country bias if we can find good quality companies throughout the world. The bottom line for us is that whether or not the UK is cheap, the US doesn't look particularly cheap and hasn't looked it for a while; big problems in relation to corporate leverage there but there are some markets that we would consider as stand out bargains and, as I say, Japan is one of them.

And there's a slightly ominous aspect to this to the extent that there's a fund manager I met in 2001 I think, and he said Japan had been the dress rehearsal, the rest of the world would be the main event. And I think what he meant by that was, Japan as the historical example is fascinating but Japan went into recession, went into depression 25 years before the rest of us. They cut rates to zero, in fact they went negative. I have an ominous feeling that the rest of the world is now slowly joining them basically 25 years after the fact.

One of the things you touched on there that I think is very relevant, particularly for people watching us who are approaching retirement, is a tendency for traditional financial managers to put you into more and more bonds the nearer to retirement you get and yet with interest rates on the rise, I'm thinking that's probably quite a dangerous place to be?

I couldn't agree more. There's some figures that I was looking at recently, they relate to the 1970s. If you were an investor in UK Government Bonds or Gilts in the early 1970s you had to wait 12 years until you got your money back. So, in other words, you suffered 12 years of negative real returns, that's after inflation. Now that's the 1970s and that's because of a protracted period of stagflation, inflation and no real economic growth.

That's the 1970s experience and it'll still be valid for some investors out there who remember suffering through that. The UK Government Bond market is now a lot more expensive than it was back then, as you said earlier, 4,000/5,000 year lows in interest rates. As interest rates slowly start to pick back up, the one iron law in finance is if interest rates go up, bond prices go down. Bonds typically have fixed coupons; they pay fixed interest, so when interest rates rise, the price of the bond falls to compensate for that.

As you also correctly say, a whole legion of investors have been advised to own bonds for risk purposes, but that's all investment strategy out of the rear view mirror, it's not looking forward, it's simply saying well 'bonds have worked since the 1980s' - just because they have worked for the last 40 years doesn't mean they're going to work for the next 4 years.

So if it's not bonds, what are we saying people should be looking to invest in in this current climate perhaps as they move towards retirement?

Well the way we're attempting to answer that question is that, within our managed accounts service, we allocate to three types of assets. We allocate to value stocks, for example the kind of stuff that we invest in within our fund. We allocate to a specific type of absolute return fund, which we call Systematic Trend Following Funds, which is a price momentum-based approach. It's completely uncorrelated to the Stock Market, completely uncorrelated to the bond market, so it's a fantastic diversifier, whatever the returns are we know those returns won't be linked to traditional asset markets. And then the third piece of the pie, we allocate to what we call real assets, but for real assets read specifically gold, silver and high quality miners of gold and silver.

I know you've long been a fan of the yellow metal as a core part of your own portfolio, is that still the case?

Absolutely, I mean gold just on its own is a topic we could discuss until the cows come home, but it strikes me that if we're living through this period of extraordinary financial uncertainty, interest rates starting to normalise finally after years of manipulation, a lot of asset markets looking a bit top heavy and lots of political problems, then I can't really think of a better portfolio hedge or an inflation hedge or a financial crisis hedge for the long run than things like gold. The one beauty of gold, unlike any other asset, is it hasn't got any counterparty or credit risk.

There's a friend of mine, Charlie Morris, who has a great line for this, he says, think of gold as a zero coupon perpetual bond, i.e. it will never expire, it has no credit risk, it has no counterparty risk and it's issued by God!

Excellent! Well we certainly do live in uncertain times as you say. I can't let you go without mentioning the dreaded B word. Now the Brexit outcome is changing all the time, but at a higher level than day-to-day events, what should investors be doing to cope with wherever Brexit takes us?

This approach didn't necessarily work last year because last year was really freakish; 2018 was a very freakish year because nothing worked basically. But notwithstanding that, 12 months isn't necessarily a period to be really fretting about things not working, we need a longer perspective than that. The one thing I generally suggest is that the one remaining free lunch in investing is diversification. So if not winning then avoiding losing - it's don't put all your assets into one particular type of asset class, so equities alone, listed stocks aren't the answer, bonds I don't think certainly are the answer. Look for slightly more flexible vehicles like say absolute return funds - we use trend following funds - a bit of everything and if you're really concerned about the implications of Brexit, then clearly you want to moderate your exposure to the UK plc and you want to moderate your exposure to sterling.

And leading on from Brexit, the other possibility of course it that we end up with a Corbyn-McDonnell government and I sense a lot of apathy about that at the moment, yet to me that's a bigger risk than Brexit.

I think you're absolutely right. There's been a dark cloud hanging over the FTSE, over UK investments for a while. I think that that cloud hanging over the market is almost entirely a function of reflecting fears about a Corbyn-McDonnell government. As one asset manager recently said, 'well I know my Trotskyites and I know that a Trotskyite government isn't good for markets', and he's absolutely right. And even the potential of having what I would consider a rabidly left wing government is it makes fears of a Brexit look like a vicarage tea party.

Yes and I think we'll be taking bets on how long it is before we go running to the IMF for a bail out.

Yes, if we were to re-enter that kind of political environment then there's a dreadful feeling that history is going to repeat itself.

Okay. Great, well that's been a fascinating discussion Tim. One of the things I want to recommend to people is that they follow your work on your blog at The Price of Everything, which if I had my way would get a Pulitzer Prize.

That's very nice, the cheque's in the post.

Thank you very much for joining us, Tim Price.

Three Key Lessons
From Tim Price

1. **The ability to convey your ideas in writing is a valuable one** – Tim has used his writing in Money Week to enhance his status as a fund manager and his experience as a fund manager to inform his writing. While he has not developed as high a media profile as Justin Urquhart Stewart, he combined writing in the specialist press and speaking at financial events to build his profile and his client base.

2. **In these uncertain times focus on avoiding losses** – this is especially true for those who have already accumulated significant wealth, but applies equally during the wealth building phase. Make sure you spread your risk across different asset classes and watch out for bond prices falling if interest rates rise and watch out for tracker funds that will follow the market down without any proactive corrective action.

3. **Look for great companies available at a price below market value** – the essence of value investing. Be prepared to look anywhere in the world to find them, for example Asia. Be ready to buy more if the price falls rather than copying the crowd who run away when high quality stocks and shares are available at bargain basement prices!

Lord Stanley Fink

Lord Stanley Fink
The 'Godfather of Hedge Funds'

Stanley Fink, Baron Fink is a hedge fund manager, formerly CEO of Man Group plc and, since 2011, a member of the House of Lords.

He started his career at the accountancy firm, Arthur Andersen and briefly worked for Mars Incorporated before joining Citibank.

He served as Chief Executive Officer of Man Group, a hedge fund, from 2000 to 2007. Described as the 'Godfather' of the UK hedge fund industry, he is credited with building the Man Group up to its current status as the largest listed hedge fund company in the world.

In September 2008, he came out of retirement to act as the Chief Executive of International Standard Asset Management (ISAM) in partnership with Lord Levy. He became Chairman of ISAM in 2015 and retired from any formal role with the company in December 2018.

In January 2009 Fink was appointed Co-Treasurer of the Conservative Party and in January 2011 was created a Life Peer. After the resignation of Peter Cruddas over a cash-for-access controversy, Lord Fink returned as Treasurer of the Conservative Party, to which he had previously donated £2.62m. He is one of the top 20 biggest donors to the Conservative Party.

Welcome to Money & Me. My guest in this chapter is known as the Godfather of the hedge fund industry, he is also a major philanthropist and investor in new businesses as well as being a contributor and former Treasurer of the Conservative Party, he is Lord Stanley Fink. Lord Fink, welcome to Money & Me.

Thank you Graham and please call me Stanley, most people do.

Thank you very much, I'll do that. Now before we talk about your highly successful career in the hedge fund industry, I want to take you back to your childhood because there's a rather well-known Prime Minister who was the daughter of a grocer in Lincolnshire and you're the son of a grocer in Manchester. What is it about growing up in a grocer's family that leads to this amazing success?

Well my father, for most of my very young life, was a manufacturer of wire lampshades that people used to cover with raffia. But he had a split from his brother and business partner and his brother bought the business and my father ended up taking his share of the proceeds and reinvesting it in the grocery business. So he was really a grocer for the latter part of his career and probably my teenage years onwards.

And in my case it was a different life because in the first business my mother had not really worked, she'd been a stay-at-home mum, but once my parents bought the grocery shop she was working full time. And we used to sometimes in the holidays go and help and I think it does give you a real hands-on experience of the real world and the customers you have and the lives they live in a way that many other businesses don't. So I think it does give you a connection with the real world.

And was the topic of money or saving or investing ever discussed around the dinner table at home?

It wasn't discussed as a sort of abstract topic but I think, as you live through the experience with the family and business and good months and bad months, you realise certain values your parents had and a certain philosophy. So, for example, my parents were savers, they had debt, they believed in mortgage debt and a minor amount of business debt at some points, but really they tried to de-gear pretty quickly and believed it was better to be a saver than a spender. Putting things aside for a rainy day was very much part of their philosophy. And I guess they grew up in an era where the welfare state wasn't as prevalent and people really did have to look out for themselves.

You went on to study law at university and then you had a variety of different roles in different companies like Arthur Andersen, Mars, Citibank; at that stage was there ever a plan as to how you wanted your career to unfold or were you opportunistically jumping between things that just looked interesting?

It's a very good question. I knew that I wanted to end up in business but I didn't specifically know which business and perhaps with the exception of saying it probably wasn't going to be the grocery business! I didn't know at the time I went to university that the subject of economics existed - my school was probably one of the last in Britain to do economics. In fact I gave an inaugural economics lecture to the pupils probably just seven or eight years ago, so it was really late. And so I'd done science up to A-Level and I really was more a scientist than a lawyer, but I thought a law degree gave me some skills I would need on my journey to become a rounded businessman. Despite not really enjoying my law degree, I do find it very useful both in many of the businesses I've been involved in and also as a Parliamentarian now. The amount of legislation one reads, I don't know how people without legal training understand what they're actually reading.

So you then landed at Man Group which got you started in the hedge fund business at a time when most people wouldn't have known what a hedge fund was. How did that all come about and where did you take it?

It was serendipity. I joined Man having worked with them when they were a banking client of mine. I was at Citibank, and I really liked the firm. I spent an intensive period with them looking at how they would pass on the firm from the old generation to the younger generation by effectively selling the business but in reality doing a leverage buy-out or, in this case, buy-in. And I really got to know the Managers and in order to prepare the credit they needed I really had to understand the business.

I think they were impressed with what they saw and they offered me a job shortly after the exercise finished, even though the exercise never ultimately happened, but we did get credit approval from the bank! I felt that it was the sort of business that was young and dynamic. At the time most of its businesses were in the commodity sector - agricultural commodities: coffee, cocoa, sugar, and indeed the commodity business still exists today but as an independent company. I joined them in a financial role.

I was fortunate then to get involved in a couple of large transactions that helped grow the company and then I became the Chief Financial Officer and I helped float the company in 1994. It was only after the IPO (*Initial Public Offering – GR*) that I was asked to do a sideways move in effect to become the head of its rather small hedge fund business.

Ah right because a lot of people bandy this term around without really understanding it. Could you help me by defining what a hedge fund is and how it differs from a regular investment?

Sure, my definition, though I've not really checked it would be a universal one, but for me a hedge fund is a fund that is going to look for an absolute return not a return relative to an index. It's a fund that can go short of markets as well as long, it can use leverage and derivatives in a way that many standard mutual funds can't, and it generally has management who are motivated through incentive fees so that they are aligned with their clients.

So those are the typical characteristics, but the range of instruments and strategies are just enormous. The type I was mainly involved with were funds that traded the futures markets, which were historically commodities, but nowadays interest rates, stock indices, even emission derivatives are part of what a modern CTA (*Commodity Trading Advisors – GR*) type hedge fund trades.

But of course not all hedge funds have been as successful as they hoped or achieved their goal, so if someone's thinking about investing in a hedge fund what are the kind of characteristics they need to look for?

For me, if one is looking at a personal level rather than going through a consultant, and there are consultants who advise on this as there are on many other subjects, for me one of the key things is to look for a strategy where management can articulate what they're doing. I've met many hedge funds where you speak to them and they cannot actually explain to you in words that make sense, what their strategy is! So make sure the strategy makes sense, make sure that there's some sort of track record or experience, have an understanding of the biggest loss that both has occurred and could theoretically occur, and ideally look at the way that the performance of that hedge fund fits the rest of your portfolio.

One of the reasons I've always liked the managed futures area is it tends to have a very low correlation to both the stock market and indeed things like the property market. So it often does very well in bear markets because it can go short equally as well as it can go long of the markets.

And I guess a lot of people think we're heading for a fairly turbulent time in the markets, so does that mean potentially for the right kind of hedge fund there's actually going to be some rich pickings in the next few years?

I think there will always be rich pickings for people of certain styles. If the markets really go into a bear market then CTA managers who follow trends like the one I work with, ISAM, (*a specific hedge fund specialising in systematic investing and trend following strategies – GR*) would do very well in that sort of market. If the markets are more range bound (*staying broadly at the same level rather than rapidly rising or falling – GR*) then it would be different strategies that we do well. But no, there will almost certainly be a hedge fund type that does well in virtually every market scenario, it's just making sure you're in the right type at the right time or looking at what, over time, makes good returns.

Is that almost the equivalent of stock picking or can you take a single diversified hedge fund where you could benefit from all those strategies in a single entity?

The only type of hedge fund that really can benefit in all market strategies are 'funder funds' or multi-strategy funds, and they do have issues because there can be two levels of fees etc. Individual hedge funds tend to do well in most market conditions but there's very few that can do well in all market conditions.

Okay, but if we take that period when you were running Man Group, what would be the typical kind of annual returns investors were experiencing?

Man Group, in our average retail product, particularly the ones focused around AHL, the main product (*a quantitative or quant fund – GR*), they would typically have been earning 15% to 20% returns with about a 15% to 20% annualised volatility, so a Sharpe Ratio of about 0.8 to 1% in terms of risk return (*Sharpe Ratio is a means of examining the performance of an investment by adjusting for its risk - GR*).

So Stanley, once you've achieved that level of success, its one thing to kind of make money in business but then it's a case of how do I transform that into long term wealth? What were the kind of processes you went through to move from that 'high income phase' into the 'investing for the long term phase'?

It's a good question. I think my philosophy was very much driven by wanting to spend the balance of my life doing something really meaningful for society. I'm very fortunate that I've got three wonderful, well-adjusted children who all have good independent careers of their own. I was able to have a portfolio that I knew was pretty balanced and safe and conventional, but I wanted to invest in new business because its business and new business that fascinates me, particularly businesses that can have a social and utilitarian purpose as well as making money and making returns, because by doing that you can recycle the capital.

So I'm interested in a range of businesses which vary from some very green businesses like New Forest Capital which is focused on renewable forestry, and businesses that measure the impact of human activity on the planet. One example is a business called Ecometrica that really does that by helping companies measure the impact of their carbon footprint etc. I'm invested in a number of businesses that supply things that are really important like Etopia, which is looking at new ways to build homes in more affordable greener ways and in businesses like British Pearl, which helps bring a new way for individuals to invest in the property market and get their foot in the property market without the having to have the sum of money or the time to manage their property investments personally in a way that a buy-to-let landlord would have done. So it's really finding that balance.

And I guess, although obviously you're looking for some kind of social angle there, at the end of the day it's still an investment decision and you come very much from a finance and investment background. So how do you go about assessing the propositions that are put in front of you and deciding which are the ones you are actually going to go for?

It's a very good question. After realising one or two investments, I did share some of my wealth around the family. And I'm fortunate in that my eldest son, and more recently my younger son, work in the financial world as well. And it was actually my eldest son, Alex's idea to have a Family Investment Club, where we literally looked at investments together and made decisions together where we would invest.

And while there will be some investments that perhaps I'll do that they won't because my pockets are deeper and perhaps my risk tolerance is higher, it's a really fascinating process to hear from them about the sort of businesses they want to invest in and see the way they operate. You get to see your children as grown up businessmen in their own right, whereas actually most of the other ways you interact with your children you end up seeing them like children even though they're, in my case, in their 20s and 30s!

So it's been a really nice experience both from a social interaction point of view as well as helping us get enthusiastic together about businesses.

Okay, now I think people always tend to be very quick to tell others about their successful investments but I would imagine not everything has gone according to plan. Have there been one or two of these that just didn't work out?

Absolutely. As I once said to my wife when two or three of the early investments we made didn't go well, I said to her 'lemons suddenly ripened faster than plums'. Unfortunately it was true, we did have a couple of plums ripen, but we've also had a number of investments that didn't work out for a variety of reasons, either over-optimism by the management or a factor we'd ignored, the competitive factor or a critical mass issue. And the important thing there is to recognise failure early, to have an open and frank dialogue with management and to decide in advance what your risk tolerance is.

I think that the biggest mistakes I've made with hindsight is continuing to fund investments hoping they'll turn around with a bit more money. While showing support to the investments you make, and I've never been somebody who cuts and runs at the first sign of adversity, you have to explain what your criteria would be to reinvest, and try to help them through the difficult times because all businesses have some difficult times. But you need the discipline at a certain point to say 'enough is enough'.

The areas where I kick myself are those where I carried on too long and there are probably one or two of those. They are things I think probably, of all the things in our marriage, my wife berates me about the most!

Okay, let's talk about one of the success stories, which is British Pearl. We've got a whole generation now that feels like they're struggling to get on the property ladder, but I suppose this sort of platform offers them a way of getting into the property investing world without necessarily having to afford an entire property themselves?

It does, British Pearl is a really good way for people to take an exposure to property that's appropriate for their overall portfolio. But if you think about it, most people live most of their lives short of property, either they're not on the property ladder and they can see it going up and they get frustrated by it, or they're in a house but they know at some point the family is going to grow and they're going to need to buy a bigger house.

And the problem is, having been in both positions, in a rising market it's very painful that, as you make savings, the property you might want to buy goes up in price more than your savings. And particularly if you look at a year like this, where the Stock Market is probably down about 10% on the year (*the interview was recorded in late 2018 - GR*), if you've saved in the year in stocks, if you've bought low risk ISAs you'll probably make 2% in your year. On the British Pearl platform today you can make over 4% tax free in an ISA in a loan product through them, plus any equity – the properties are only put on the platform when they're pre-let – so there's probably been an 8% to 10% return in terms of income and capital gain in properties where you invest in the equity of British Pearl properties. And that's all secured by a property; it could in theory go to zero but it would have to mean the property is worthless, so it's relatively safe as an investment strategy.

Somebody smarter than me once said 'it ain't what you make that matters it's what you keep'. And that brings us onto a three letter swear word spelled T-A-X. Now there have been a lot of changes, many of them introduced by your Party, under Mr Osborne, like Section 24, that have really kind of impacted people in recent years. In fact I think the House of Lords recently said that perhaps the powers of HMRC have gone too far. What's you view on where things have been going with the Conservative Government and its general approach to tax, tax planning and tax avoidance in recent years?

I think some of the changes to root out some of the most artificial avoidance by changing legislation is sensible, but I think that we should be very clear as a society to separate tax evasion, which is absolutely illegal from tax avoidance, which has become a dirty word. And perhaps it's fair when there are schemes that are particularly artificial but actually it's one of those difficult subjective words because most people who write a Will or do estate planning - you could argue that's tax avoidance. You could even argue that buying your whisky as you cross over an airport, duty free, is tax avoidance because all things being equal, it would easier to pick up your whisky from your local supermarket and pay tax on it. So I think one has got to be very careful. My personal view is if people think things are wrong they should change the law and try and not do it retrospectively. And that's very much how I was brought up.

I think some of the problems that the House of Lords was talking about in the balance, is probably to do with the merger between the Inland Revenue and Her Majesty's Customs & Excise, because the Customs & Excise have always had wider powers and probably been more aggressive historically. I think it's the combination of those two that has led to the specific situation that was spoken about. But that's something that in political terms is well above my pay grade to comment about. But most of my dealings over the years with the Inland Revenue, most of the time they've been very fair to deal with.

As we come to the end of our time together, from your experience of a lifetime in the financial and investment industry, what would be the golden nougats you'd want to pass onto people that you've learned in your career?

I think in terms of investment I'd say diversify, don't put all your eggs in one basket. Don't think because you've got a lot of equities it's great because equities have in the past gone down and stayed down for quite a long time. Having an element of bonds or cash, an element of property either directly or through a vehicle like British Pearl is a good thing. So diversification is the nearest thing to a free lunch you get in a financial market. (*Not the first person to use that expression! GR*)

I also think you make a living by what you earn but you build a life by what you give (*we need to credit Churchill with that one! – GR*). So some of the most emotionally rewarding things I've had are to be involved in some major philanthropic projects, and to particularly involve my children in some with me along the way. That's been a great journey and I've met some remarkable people, both in terms of the practitioners who help people within the charitable projects and also some of my fellow donors who I've met - people I would not have met in my normal business life.

Perfect, well that's a great way to end our time together. Lord Stanley Fink, thank you very much for joining us.

Thank you Graham.

Three Key Lessons
From Lord Stanley Fink

1. **Your client can become your employer** – Lord Fink's big break came after he had done some work for Man Group as a client and they liked what they saw. Whether you are an employee or a service provider, keep your antennae tuned for an opportunity to further your career (provided you do not breach any No Poaching agreements!)

2. **Set up a Family Investment Company** to involve the next generation in managing the wealth you have created. This can also be a highly tax efficient means of passing wealth between the generations if it is structured correctly from the start. Make sure you receive advice from a tax planning expert – do not rely on a High Street accountant to know all the tweaks that will make a big difference to your long term wealth.

3. **Understand the importance of philanthropy** – Many people only consider this when they have made their fortune, but you will find deep satisfaction in giving even more modest amounts while working to accumulate wealth. You will also bump into people in the charity world that can help in your business and investing life. The bible says that you will be richly rewarded when you give – most are cynical. Until they try it…

Section 2

The Entrepreneurs

Jonathan Jay

James Sinclair

The Marquess of Bristol

Luke Lang

Jonathan Jay

Jonathan Jay

Jonathan Jay is one of the world's leading trainers on buying and selling businesses, with a 20 year plus track record of high performance companies and multi-million pound exits.

Over the last 20 years Jonathan has bought companies from private equity firms and sold companies to private equity firms – he has made trade deals and snapped up bust competitors and merged them with businesses already in his portfolio.

Jonathan is also the author of eight business books.

He has been featured on CNBC, presented TV shows for the BBC and been interviewed for Forbes magazine. His business mentoring day rate of £10,000 was reported in the Guardian and he was the featured Entrepreneur in The Financial Times.

Jonathan runs seminars to teach business owners how to grow faster via acquisition and how entrepreneurially minded people can buy their competitors or other businesses. He is also an active business investor himself and is currently involved in the children's nursery sector.

Jonathan lives between Marbella and London.

See more at www.thedealmakersacademy.com and get a free copy of his latest book, *"How to Buy and Sell Great Businesses - Without Risking Your Own Money"*.

My guest in this chapter is one of the Britain's most prolific entrepreneurs, he's bought and sold 25 companies in the last 20 years and made a significant amount of money in the process. His name is Jonathan Jay; Jonathan welcome to Money & Me.

Thank you.

Now it seems the entrepreneur gene struck quite early; I think you had your first business card at the age of 11?

I did.

What was that all about?

Well my hobby was doing magic tricks, conjuring, so I had a magic show that I sold to parents and I did birthday parties for 4 year olds, 5 year olds, 6, 7, 8, 9, sometimes 10 years olds - sometimes they were actually close to my age, which was a bit odd! Everyone thought I was older than I was but I needed a business card, I needed promotional material. I advertised in the local newspaper every Friday and I ran it like a proper business and actually did a lot of the things that many business owners don't do even decades after. But it came very instinctively, I enjoyed it, I enjoyed the thrill of building the business and yeah, that was the start.

So how did that come about, was it something to do with the family environment that you were brought up in that encouraged that kind of entrepreneurial spirit?

Not really, I had a magician at my birthday party when I was 6 or 7 and that was what inspired me to be interested in that subject. My parents always had their own business; they had a dance school, so they always worked for themselves. I don't think they necessarily considered it as a business, more of a self-employed status and there is a psychological difference if nothing else. It was a modest business but I didn't ever see my parents walk out the door at 9 o'clock in the morning and come home at 5 o'clock, there was never that regularity. And I've never had the regularity in my life either, it's always been a little bit more exciting shall we say.

So was money ever discussed around the dinner table in the family?

No, never and if it was it was typically lack of money! It wasn't a particularly affluent environment, I don't think we ever went without food or clothes, not to that extreme. We had holidays but it certainly wasn't the environment where money was talked about openly, which I think is something that I'd want to do differently with my children.

You say you've had an exciting life -have you ever had a proper job working for someone else?

The closest I have ever got is as a student, where I worked as a demonstrator, a magician demonstrator in Harrods and Hamley's on Saturdays and Wednesdays - that was the closest I got to having a payslip and a pay cheque every month. That was for a couple of years on and off, but apart from that I've never ever worked for anyone else.

Then you went to university and started studying French but I think you got a bit bored with that after a while didn't you?

Well I didn't really want to do French, I just landed with a French degree because I couldn't get into the course I wanted. So I did it a little bit reluctantly and then realised that I wanted to do my own thing. It was a four year degree – I didn't want to spend four years studying something I wasn't that interested in, so I quit after a year and started doing my own thing.

And what was that? What was your first business enterprise as a grown up?

You really want to know?

Yes!

I don't often talk about this Graham. So for five years I worked, and I don't think you know this, I worked as a professional stage hypnotist.

Wow.

I toured all the universities in the UK, so I just specialised in the university student union market because the person who taught me, that was what he did. So I sold myself into the universities. This was pre-internet, pre-home computing to a certain degree, I had all the names and telephone numbers of the university student unions on file cards. 9 o'clock in the morning I'd start phoning and I would put the cards into different piles according to whether I had to phone them back later or not until next week, and I would just phone, sell myself on the phone, sell the show on the phone. Then I'd send off the contract, typed with a typewriter, get it back in the post in the stamped, addressed envelope and I was doing okay. I think I was doing about £100,000 a year - this was 25 years ago as a 21 year old selling myself into the unis.

Wow, that's a brilliant model but I suppose ultimately not very scalable if you're also the one having to go on stage.

Well that was the issue because if I didn't work I didn't get paid! And on one particular occasion I was unwell, which doesn't happen very often but I was ill, possibly self-induced illness and I couldn't work. I couldn't do the show and if I couldn't do the show I didn't get paid, so it was actually a lousy business model and that's what made me realise that I needed a business that made in income even when I wasn't there.

Okay, so having the realisation is one thing, but then having the smarts to find such a business is quite another. What process did you go through and what kind of business did you end up in?

Well it wasn't particularly scientific, I just wanted to be in business and I didn't really mind what business it was but it actually made sense to do something that I was familiar with, a market that I understood. I understood student unions and I understood how the entertainment in student unions was booked and I realised that every student union I went to had filing cabinets full of rather average marketing material for bands, comedians, all the things that you would have in a student union or at summer balls and Christmas balls. So I put together a magazine, where I could sell advertising space to all the people who would normally send materials through the post to student unions. I sold them advertising space and then sent that magazine free of charge to all of the student unions, very similar to what Richard Branson did with his student magazine when he was a student.

And he seemed to do okay with it.

He did alright yeah.

How did yours go?

Well not so well, because I realised that the people placing the advertising were terrible at paying their bills, so I was always owed lots of money and I had all my costs upfront, so again it wasn't a great model but it taught me a lot.

Oh I see, but I think from that you then became one of the first and most successful people to bring the whole concept of coaching into the UK?

Yes.

How did you break through the apathy because I've often found that Brits are very reluctant to accept the need for coaching?

Yes, this was 1998/99. Today, I sit in a Costa Coffee and hear people talking about coaching, and not sports coaching, I'm talking about executive coaching, business coaching, life coaching, which you never would have heard 20 years ago. But I was on an exhibition stand with another one of my magazine titles, which was a corporate hospitality magazine, because they were better at paying their bills, but it was more competitive, so again wasn't a great business model. And I was on this stand for three days opposite an American coaching company. And it was a very quiet exhibition and as tends to happen at quiet exhibitions, you speak to everyone else because there's no one else to speak to. So I'm speaking to the other exhibitors and they said 'well we're part of this American coaching university' I think they called it, and I said well why did you go to America, why didn't you do it in the UK, and they said well no one does it in the UK. And I found out that they charged, I think it was $3,000, which was about £2,000 at the time. So I had another magazine in my little stable of titles, which was on personal development, I went to all the people who wrote articles for me on personal development and said 'could you run a coaching course?', I'll go and find the clients, you put together the training programme and it will be a winning combination. So, as a result of that, we did our first training programme in October 1999, just about 20 years ago. It was a storming success that changed my financial life in one weekend. I went from having nothing, lots of credit card debt and not being able to pay my mortgage - I mean it was pretty critical really - but I went from £0 to £20,000 in the bank across the course of a week. My bank manager was on holiday that week, he phoned me up when he got back and said 'Jonathan, what's happening, something must have happened in the last week, you've gone from -20 to +20, what's happening?' And that was the very first training course and I ran those training courses every month for seven years and then sold the company to a private equity firm!

Fantastic! So your business career got off to a flying start when you sold the coaching business. Now let's turn to what you've really made your name as, which is as a buyer and seller of lots of different companies. So Jonathan, is it a case that having sold those first few businesses, you got a taste for the deal rather than perhaps for simply running businesses the way most people do?

Well what most people do is they say that they own a business, and technically they do, they own the shares in the company. However, they actually live their lives as business operators, so they fulfil a management role. Now that's a very important role in a business but I don't think it should be the role conducted by the owner of the business because it's very limiting. It means that you spend your day answering the phone, creating invoices, signing for deliveries, changing the ink in the photocopier machine and all of these types of operational activities, where the real skill that a business owner should have is an investor in businesses and growing their company, perhaps by acquisition. And I learnt that I could make more money selling a business than I could from running a business. I could grow my business and double its value, and with the coaching business that we talked about, I doubled its value and I added millions to the value by acquiring competitors. And I didn't actually spend very much acquiring those competitors, but instead of just taking little bunny hops in my business, like hiring another advertising person, or another salesperson, I took huge kangaroo leaps and I made millions more as a result. And you know what, it wasn't difficult, in actual fact it was very easy, it was fun and it wasn't stressful!

Wow, so I think in a sense this was a revelation for you and it's now one that you try and help other people to achieve by coaching them in how to go around buying and selling businesses.

Yes I do that one day a week. So one day of every week is blocked out to help other business owners do what I do and what I have done. And I either do that in a group setting or I do it on a one-to-one basis. But I spend 20% of the working week helping other people and I spend four days of the working week doing it myself.

OK, so obviously you spend a lot of time with business owners. What are the kind of mistakes you see them making that ultimately will have a detrimental impact on their long-term wealth?

Oh that's a very good question and extremely relevant because I was actually with two people wanting to sell their business to me yesterday afternoon. And, as I was listening to them, I realised that the attitude of the owner of a business will influence their exit value. And the attitude that is typically missing that devalues the business for them is having focus and clarity. And when a business owner has focus and clarity about what they do, who they sell to and why people should buy from them, it actually increases the value of their business. First, because they have a better business and it runs with more focus and clarity and therefore more successfully and more profitably. And second, when you are selling your business, if you can't explain to someone why they should buy your business quite frankly, why should they buy it? I meet five or six business owners every week who want to sell, so I hear the same things again and again and again and what I look for is that clarity of purpose.

Great, that's an important point for anyone watching us that wants to sell their business. Now obviously in doing all these deals you've managed to make a few bob, what sorts of investments have you made outside of the business world to secure that long-term wealth?

I've only ever made one investment and that's in property. I started doing this just the way many people do - when you move house you don't sell the old house you rent it out and then you move again and you keep the next one and you rent it out. And so I became the accidental landlord. And what I didn't have, which I would encourage anyone to get, is an education in how to invest, because I just made it up as I went along so I made lots of mistakes. I made some poor decisions that I could have avoided with the right level of education and I just muddled my way through it with not much of a strategy, but still I acquired a decent sized portfolio over the years. It then shrunk again and now it's growing again. I don't know much about other things but I understand property really through trial and error, but if someone had taught me how to do it, I would have been a lot smarter.

Interesting. I believe one of the aspects that comes into some of the business deals you do is that if there's a commercial property attached to the business, suddenly that gives you a few more options?

Yes absolutely. I have several property investors who are clients and they're looking at businesses not just for the operational business but for the property angle as well. So maybe it's an MOT test centre that comes with a large site and a profitable business, maybe it's a pub type business where you've got an investment where in the future you can develop it and turn it into flats, whatever it might be. So there are two angles - a business and a property investment playing in parallel with each other.

Okay understood. So is there any particular investment mistake you'd own up to that people watching us might learn from?

There's probably been so many it's hard to select! I can give you a broad mistake that I've certainly made and I see other people make, which is where you get emotionally attached to an investment. You do it because you want the stroking of your ego, it feels like something you can brag about rather than something that's backed up by common sense and numbers. And I see people saying 'I really want to buy that business' and they can't actually justify why they should buy it but they know that they want it. And I've probably pursued things irrationally and typically the less rational you are, the more emotional you are, the poorer the decision-making is.

Yes absolutely. Is there anything that keeps you awake at night, is it Brexit, is it politics, what worries you?

Well rather selfishly I pay more attention to my own personal economy than the economy of a country that really I can't influence too much. So I do sleep very well at night, but if I was to worry or be concerned it's because I know what not having any money is like, I know what it's like to be completely broke. So I always have this fear of loss, so I keep on going, I never want to stop so I never talk about retirement, I never talk about early retirement. When people say 'when are you going to hang your hat up?', I love what I do, why should I stop doing something that I love doing? And it's not really about the money, it's about a benchmark, it's about the game if you like.

Okay lovely. Now you relatively recently became a father, what do you intend to teach your daughter about finance and at what sort of age do you think you'll start that conversation?

Well I think it's being comfortable with money and not telling your children that money is a bad thing or it's the route of all evil and all these phrases that can set people along the wrong path. And it's certainly not about worshipping money but it's about respecting the fact that the money that you earn is a reflection of the value that you bring. The more value you bring the more people return that with money that you can then do other things with. And it's about creating security, it's about giving yourself choices, it's about giving your family choices, giving your friends choices, it's about having choice and freedom.

Okay but I suppose what I'm getting at is, you know she will inherit a lifestyle that's a lot more prosperous than you did when you were a child, and is there a way in which you have to try and avoid that changing her in any sort of negative way?

I think again, it's about the environment that you grow up in, about keeping your feet on the ground and realising that just because you have money or you have access to money doesn't make you a special person. It just means that you've been fortunate and you should respect the fact that you've been fortunate and put it to work. I do think that learning the basics of investing is absolutely essential to any child.

Finally – our time together has shot by incredibly quickly – you said you're not ready for retirement, what's left on the Jonathan Jay bucket list of things you want to do in life?

Oh several lifetimes worth of things. I'm learning every day, there's always something exciting round the corner, I've always got several balls in the air at any one point. So every year the answer to that question will be different, but I'm certainly not going to stop any time soon.

Brilliant, thanks very much for the pearls of wisdom you've shared with us today Jonathan.

My pleasure!

Three Key Lessons
From Jonathan Jay

1. **You make more money when you sell a business than when you operate it** – develop the mentality of a business investor rather than a business operator and focus on creating a saleable business with a ready made management team that works without you

2. **Grow through acquisition rather than organically** – this will enable you to grow in kangaroo jumps rather than bunny hops as a single deal could double the size of your business in an afternoon. Jonathan runs a whole programme on this at the Dealmakers Academy

3. **Don't retire from something you love!** Friends and family may ask you when you are going to slow down but why should you if you are happy? Retirement is a dangerous concept unless you have a clear idea of what you want to 'retire to'. Most people spend their lives doing things they don't enjoy – if you're lucky enough to find a business or career that is fulfilling keep at is as long as you can!

James Sinclair

James Sinclair

James Is The Founder And CEO Of The Partyman Group of Companies. He started his career entertaining as 'Jimbo the Partyman' aged 15, built up an entertainment agency, then moved into acquiring his first soft play venue, laser arenas, day nursery and outdoor venues.

Today James operates a £12 million business which includes leisure, childcare, outdoor attractions, a web-based soft toy business as well as a training business, Success Seminars.

His companies have achieved £100 million in sales and welcome over a million customers through their doors every year. He also likes to help business owners learn from the highs and lows of his own journey through daily podcasts, videos, keynote speaking and books.

James's business empire includes 9 indoor leisure units, 3 laser arenas, 5 day nurseries, a 50 acre farm park attraction, a water park and a company that has made over a million teddy bears - Teddy Tastic. The diverse range of businesses have been strategically developed to complement each other through the annual seasonal peaks and troughs, dry and wet days; as well as term time and holiday periods. His three books are :

The Millionaire Clown - a business survival guide of the James' rules for success.

The Experience Business - Not just a customer service book but a book about the rules a business needs to have to deliver consistent customer service.

Getting Customers. For acquiring customers faster, easier and with less money than you ever thought possible.

You can learn more at jamessinclair.net

My guest in this chapter started his first business at just 15 years of age and he now runs a company that turns over £10 million and employs over 400 people. The way he got started can be hinted at by the title of his best-selling book, 'Millionaire Clown'; his name is James Sinclair. James welcome to Money & Me.

Thanks very much; interesting listening to your little bio of me there!

Well I'm fascinated, I'm always interested in how people get started, so if we go back a bit what kind of family environment was it that led to you wanting to become an entrepreneur and an entertainer as young as 15 years of age?

I think I just wanted to start a business, I loved entertainment and I dreamed about starting a business at 13 or 14 years old - I was good at entertainment and I had this natural entrepreneurial bug. I loved finding out about how businesses worked, I used to – sad as it was as a teenager – dream about what uniforms would look like, what offices would look like, branding, how to market, how to get customers and I just got on with it as soon as I could. And so I started a little entertainments business and then that grew and grew and grew and grew into where we are now.

But was there something about the family; were your parents entrepreneurs, where does that gene come from?

No not at all really. I think there's a natural talent or a natural DNA that makes someone an entrepreneur, some people have a management DNA, some people have an entrepreneurial DNA. I think I had that and then I just put it to work. And then as the years trundled on you just get better and better at things. But I think it's a base talent thing or it's a thing that's in you.

And was that in a sense symbolic of the fact that you were not massively engaged with the education system at the time?

You know I thought school was a waste of time for me, it hasn't helped me in my career. I've learned to read and write, which obviously is an important thing. I just took what I could from that and invested my time more wisely in building a business. When I was at school, I left at 16; I already had quite a good trading business. By the time I was 17 we were doing £1,500/£2,000 a week.

That was a good income at that sort of age; you must have felt like a king!

Well I didn't just spend it all, I kept putting it into property and investing in growing the business. I was seriously working for 7 days a week full time. I really did sacrifice my youth and invested that time into growing the business, which I don't necessarily think is the right thing to do but I would never have done it any other way even now. I regret not investing time into having holidays and nights out, doing all the things that other people my age did; I was more focused on building a property business, building an entertainment business, building really where I wanted to get to. I am spectacularly lucky to know what I want to achieve, whereas a lot of people struggle with that. I know where I want to be in five years, I knew at 18 that I wanted to own visitor attractions and I looked at what were the steps to doing that. First build an entertainments business, then leverage that up, buy a property then grow the security and the equity in the property to then remortgage it to go build a chain of what would be brick and mortar businesses.

So are you telling me that whilst you were working all these hours as a children's entertainer, you've also got a part of your brain that's now working on building a property empire? When did you get your first property?

When I was 18.

18 wow!

And then another one when I was 19, another one when I was 20, so I had this buy a property a year approach by saving as much as you can for the deposits. But then, when I was buying property it was all about being able to give it back to the bank as security to build my trading business, because I knew the things that I was attracted to were going to need capital. So if I wanted to own a zoo or a farm park or day nurseries or building family entertainment centres, I knew I'd need capital and I just knew I wouldn't be the sort of person who'd go down the venture capital route or something like that.

It's a big step between working on your own as both the business owner and the performer and then at some point starting to think about how you're going to build this because scalability is a bit of an issue when you're the owner and the performer...

Yeah.

So where did your thinking get you in terms of how I take that next step from being a solopreneur into building more of a company?

I just get rid of things that I don't like doing instantly. The second I was 17 I employed a cleaner because I moved out, I left home really young, my mum died so I had nothing, so I thought right let's get out there. I need to do more sales and marketing, so I employed a cleaner so I didn't have to look after the house. And then, when I was 18, I had an administrator so I didn't have to do any paperwork so I could really focus on sales and marketing, build a business rather than run a business and that was just ingrained in my head.

Most people really put off employing people when they go into starting a business. I couldn't wait to employ people to fill in the gaps that I was wasn't good at and I do that now to this day.

So what were the businesses you went into because I think, from previous conversations we've had, not all of them worked out the way you might have liked?

Yes, it's what I teach entrepreneurs when people come to my seminars or if I help entrepreneurs, I say you must fold everything you do into existing empires. So if you look at my portfolio of businesses, my day nurseries are within our indoor play centres, so they feed off each other. My farm park or my theme park, we will put in childcare that feeds off of that. We also make teddy bears, we make about half a million teddy bears a year that we sell in leisure attractions, but we're the biggest customer of that and we sell them in our attractions. So we always make sure that it's like an ecosystem that everything that we do has to feed the other parts.

We did have a chain of party shops, that was really tough you know with rents, rates, low margins - all the things I've learnt that I will never do again. It did feed into our business but we cut them off as soon as we realised this is just too hard to do. And then we had a stretch limousine company that was a bit of a disaster. We could get the customers for it but we always had to get new customers all the time because people only want to hire you out once or once every five years.

And so now I have a list of rules that dictate what I want to do. I want residual income, I want decent margins, I want low labour to turnover ratio, I want repeat customers if possible, I want higher profit sales as well as repeat sales. So I've got all these things in my head that dictate decisions, which I've only learnt from mucking other stuff up.

Right I see. Something like nurseries must be an absolute heaven from a repeat business point of view because once you get the little brat you've got them for 3-4 years?

4 years yes.

So that must have become almost a bedrock of that residual income rule?

Yes but they're quite a high labour business so I've learnt to look for businesses that have residual income, regular income, good transactional value from the customer. For a business to be successful it needs to have high average customer value or higher average transactional value. So in a supermarket, the margin is low on each item but you transact with it sometimes two or three times a week, but definitely once a week you're buying food. So that's a good business because the transactional value of the customer is high.

Now if you don't have high transactional value you need to make sure you've got high average customer value and if you can get them both then you're onto a great win/win situation. For example, Apple would have both, Disney would have both. People would subscribe to Disney channels, then they go on holidays, so they have high ACV (*average customer value – GR*) stuff and the high average transactional value and that's why they're two of the most profitable companies in the world in my opinion.

But also I think what you're hinting at there is that you need to know your numbers as a business owner and be on top of them. And I know from my own experience of my own businesses and from working with others, not that many business owners are on top of their numbers!

One of the first people that I employed was a bookkeeper and that makes a huge difference because what lots of people do is get their accountants to do a bookkeeping role and that's just stupid. You need your accountant to give you tax advice and strategic planning, raising finance and that stuff, but for the core numbers within the business a great bookkeeper, which is not expensive compared to an accountant, can really start training you up to have the basic understanding. Because you don't know until you know, and that's why people don't do it.

So we employ an FD (*Finance Director – GR*) now, so we've effectively got an in-house accountant. This gives us another level up of stuff that can really help us and you learn by being around these people. You know the classic (*Jim Rohn – GR*) phrase, 'you become the average of the five people you spend most of your time with', so if you surround yourself with great people then great things will happen.

But a lot of people will be reading this and they'll be going 'well its alright for him to say you know, that he's got this turnover, he's got all this stuff' but the first step to actually having the thing, you know I'm going to employ an accountant, I'm going to have a bookkeeper, I'm going to employ an administrator, a PA or a manager, is allowing yourself to say 'I am going to do that, I might not be able to do it today but I am certainly going to do that'. And then you start building a business that allows you to have these great people come into your organisation.

Okay, and then that puts you in charge of the numbers and you become the orchestra leader.

Most people do not want to put great people into their organisation, they just adopt this attitude of 'no we're not employing people'. I was asking myself 'how can I afford to get these people in and get them in as quick as possible?'

And it is actually a false economy to do without them isn't it because you spend all your time running around trying to do your bookkeeping at the end of a busy day, its not what you want.

I get really cross when I find business owners doing their own books. You've got to look at them and read them and understand them but don't put them together!

So how often do you review the numbers in your businesses?

I'm checking them all the time and every day I check average customer value, labour to turnover ratio, they're the two ones that I'm really focused on. Average Customer Value and labour to turnover ratio because in most businesses the biggest cost walks on two legs, so we want to be checking.

You know, it is very smart for a business to say, 'right our percentage labour to turnover is this for our sector, we need to benchmark against that' - so for retail it's 13%, for leisure 25%, for care homes and childcare 50%. You need to know where you're at and make sure you're tracking it. Because if your management accounts are produced monthly for example, a monthly profit and loss that tells you how well your business is doing is usually produced monthly - you could be 30 days after the fact when there's a problem. All you need is a simple spreadsheet that's telling you what people are spending - count your customers every day, divide that by your turnover and you want to be making sure your ACV is always going up and keep your labour on the right level. Don't go under because you'll give bad customer service, don't go over or you won't be in service!

You just want to decide what it is and keep it on a nice level playing field.

And then if you're watching those metrics, I guess every new decision is made against trying to improve those core metrics in the business?

Yes and I think that's why when you go into supermarkets now, you go into McDonald's, Costa Coffee, anything like that, they're putting in self-serve because that's bringing their labour ratios down.

So we've learned about how you've built up your business empire and how you tightly control it by focusing on some key metrics. But now James, I want to try and broaden the conversation to what happens outside the business. I know you've always had a very clear strategy about wanting to effectively make money in the business and then take it out and invest it in property, so tell us about your fast pound/slow pound strategy.

Yes I think property is a great thing to invest in but I always say business first, property second. If you can get a trading business that's doing really well it will allow you to cash flow your property stuff. And I class a business as fast pounds and property or other assets as slow pounds - whether that's stocks and shares or property or investing in other people's businesses, you know they will build up over time.

So whatever you earn, see if you can invest 50% into slow pounds and live on the other 50%. Let me explain what I mean by this. You bring in a salary, it comes in and by the end of the month it's gone for most people and if anything they need more than what they bring in. So it comes in fast, it goes out fast, so I call it fast pounds.

What I say is look, how can you get into a situation where 50% of your fast pounds you invest and 50% you live on? The average salary in the UK is about £24,000 right now, that's gross so say you've got £10,000 as 50% of your net. People say 'well I can't live on £10,000, its just not possible'. If they work up in London they need £6,000 just for travel and this is just not possible. So I'm saying you need to up your game and bring in another income stream so that you can invest into what I like, that is property. And so you invest in them and then the cash that spins off should fund the fun in life. If you want to buy a nice car or you want to go on really good holidays your slow pound building assets, i.e. for me property, fund all the good fun stuff in life.

I've tried to build my business empire up by buying businesses for zero or buying failing businesses, putting my management team in, leveraging off of them to increase the cash flow that they make so we can buy more property.

Tell me about your property investment strategy; because I think you've tended to veer more towards commercial property in recent years haven't you?

You just want to model successful people and I realise people that are really wealthy in property, like Alan Sugar for example, they don't own flats and houses, they own office blocks and commercial buildings.

And you know why do they do that? We've still got a fair sized residential portfolio but we would much rather go and buy a nice decent chunky commercial freehold. I think there's huge advantages where we're sitting right now in 2019 - lower Stamp Duty, you can claim the interest back (*unlike the way section 24 has impacted residential landlords – GR*). If you can buy a commercial property that your trading business operates out of that's like double thumbs up from me because you're controlling the rent overhead from going up. There are just so many advantages to it (*see also Jonathan Jay's comments on businesses with commercial property – GR*).

So you're running a successful trading business, when you come to have some spare pounds that you want to move across into your investment strategy, what criteria do you look for in the commercial property?

The very simple criterial is I want to make sure the rent is at least, at least 10% of the purchase price. So if you're buying something for £1 million I want to make sure that we're going to have £100,000 a year rent out of it. And then we need to work to an ROI (*return on investment – GR*) calculation on what we invest our capital in. I work to a minimum of 20% ROI, so whatever your cash flow is after all costs each year divided by the capital you've put in, that includes your Stamp Duty, your legal fees, your deposits, you times that by 100 and you get your ROI.

And you know why I like 20% ROI? Because the 300 year average base rate is 6% and we're on 0.75% as of 2019 right now and everyone thinks that they won't go up. But it's a global economy. It's decided by the Bank of England but it's also global threats that dictate a lot of that and I just think I want comfort in there. Because most people who are buying property, if you really look at your ROI, most people buy at 5% and 6%. They buy in the town that they live in, they buy on the assumption it's going to be worth that much more in the future, whereas I'm always focus on the rent - rent first, capital appreciation second and don't ever change your mind on that.

What about outside of property are there any other things that you are investing in at the moment beyond bricks and mortar?

Other than our own businesses we don't invest in anyone else's businesses, any stocks and shares and quite frankly, when we want to buy property we want to buy property that our trading business operates out of. That's not always possible, we're in big shopping centres and we're not going to buy a shopping centre but, where we can we would always do that because it's very sensible to do that.

One of the things that all business owners are having to cope with is the dreaded B word and people keep talking about 'Brexit uncertainty' and so on. Is your Brexit glass half-full or half empty?

I think the future is fantastic for this country. If you look at this country's history we've always done well. I think we're the sixth largest economy in the world right now, we're predicted to drop but we'll go back up to possibly the fifth largest economy according to something I saw in the Economist.

We've got a great legal system, we've got a great banking system, we've got a fantastic City, we've got great airports. People put it down but as a global economy people trust the UK and I think that will get us through. We've got good people here, we've got good entrepreneurial people and I think the ups and downs will always come. It's just your mindset on 'well I'm going to ride this storm and do well out of it' because we actually grew our business the most in 2008 and 2009, which was technically one of the biggest recessions of the last 100 years. We did really well out of it because I thought this is an opportunity here to go and buy businesses.

I also think that, if you're in business when a thing like Brexit comes along it stops competition saying 'right we're going to go ahead and start new stuff', so you actually get some time to coast and rethink and go again. So I think that's a really good advantage coming out of it.

Did I vote remain, did I vote leave? I'm quite open about this, I was a 'central leaver'.

A central leaver, what's one of those?

I wasn't bothered either way if we remained or left - I was sort of in the middle. I was sitting on the fence but I was slightly more leave just because when I look at Europe I see problems there. You know Germany, as of February 2019 they've just gone into recession, the Italian banking crisis is about to hit and you can see all this stuff happening and I think sometimes smaller is better.

And you could argue that where we're sitting in Docklands is a great example of how Britain can reinvent and regenerate itself - this was a whole bunch of empty docks and warehouses, it's now Manhattan on Thames.

People want to be here don't they?

This is a great city and my big thing about the country is that we need to invest more into manufacturing so we can have more Dysons, more JCB. We could do that, I don't know why we don't do that, but you know they're two great companies and there could be more of them so let's do that.

I know you're very much a shrinking violet and you wouldn't want to be in the limelight, but if you were to become Prime Minister for a period of time, what would be top of your agenda for things you would change about the country?

I don't like government running stuff that they shouldn't be running. I think they should look at education, I think they should look at protection; you know armies and stuff like that.

Security.

Security, that's the one Graham, thank you for helping me there! I think they should be concentrating on that stuff, like the police. And I think they should be finding ways to invest in the longer term rather than thinking just three, four, five years ahead and if they could say 'right we're going to invest in this and this, its going to have a 20 year payback', then it will be fantastic. That's what the Germans do much better than us as a country. We think quarter-to-quarter and sometimes as a business, as an entrepreneur, you need to think where's this going to be in five, seven, eight, nine, ten years? That's why great entrepreneurs do have that sort of vision for what does the end look like and we'll give it a bit more time. But, because of the way Parliament works, everything is so short term and that's not great for things like research and development into what's next for us as a nation.

In the last few years you've started a new career as an advisor to other business owners through initially Entrepreneurs Network and now Success Seminars, what's the motivation behind that?

Well basically, I got invited to speak in a school where the staff said they had a load of kids that didn't want to do education, but they really want to learn about business so would you come in and have a chat? This was about five years ago and I loved it, so I wrote a book afterwards that could help kids, I called it the 'Millionaire Clown' because it was ironic just to say look, if you apply a certain set of rules and learn a certain subject, it doesn't matter who you are, you can actually build something quite successful.

And then other business owners asked me to help and so I speak at seminars, I run my own business training events, where I can really seriously grow people's businesses.

And people have been following me because every day I have a man follow me round with a video camera making little documentaries of me running my businesses and I teach all the stuff on there, I suppose I reveal it so that people can discover what can be done.

And what do you find when you talk to these people, what do you find is missing from the way they're running their own businesses that you are able to help them with?

The problem with most business owners, not all but most, is they 'battle plan' but don't 'war plan', and the ones that have got a war plan that then fight the right battles are always the ones that are more successful.

So the way I describe it when I look at business owners is, I quickly think is this person fighting World War 2, which had a reason or World War 1, which didn't have a reason and that's how I explain it to people. You know WW2 there was a real reason and everyone got behind it - we needed to get rid of this dictator that was a nightmare, we had lots of battles to fight but we knew why we were fighting the battles. WW1, when you look at it, no one knew why they were fighting all these battles and it became really hard work. That's like most business owners; very hard work, very stressful and they don't know why they're fighting the battles.

So they don't know where they're heading in other words?

People might have a vision and therefore other people can follow them. It's like any organisation, you get a collective group of people where the great leader has a vision. If you look at a great secondary school, it's because there's a great Head Teacher that has a vision for the school that attracts the best teachers. This then attracts the best students and the best parents that want all that to happen. But because it is tough people forget why they're doing things and then they're just getting up fighting battles every day and they don't know why.

So you're a relatively young man, you're sitting at the top of a significant business and property empire…

I'm 33 now mate.

33, so what's next, where are you going? You said you had this plan laid out, what do you see as the grand vision for the future?

Well I want to make Partyman, which is our entertainment, leisure and childcare business, into a national brand. I think we'll get it to £15 million of revenue with a £2.5 million profit in the next 20 months or so. Then, once we've got to that stage, we'll go again and we'll build it into a £30/£40 million business. Whether I'm doing that all on my own or with someone else, we'll cross that bridge, because there's some good stuff to be done there. And then I will carry on building my personal brand, which I think is really important because it attracts opportunities to invest into businesses and help more entrepreneurs and business owners really soar to success.

I guess the way you've always done it is you've put a management team in place, so you're not always dragged into the operational day-to-day of the business?

And I'm not good at it.

Right, so that leaves you time to get involved in other projects?

Yes, my keynote phrase is 'businesses that are great run on E+M=S, which is Entrepreneurship + Management = Success'. And when you look at most organisations they're either too leadership heavy or entrepreneurship heavy or too management heavy. So the problem with leaders and entrepreneurs is they go in, make a mess and managers clear it up by saying okay, there is some good stuff in there, let's carry it on, let's build it up. The other way is if it's too management driven no one ever innovates and if you don't innovate you'll evaporate.

Right, so you need the entrepreneur leading and the management team sitting behind them.

Yes, you know entrepreneurs need great management and management are driven by great entrepreneurs.

Well that's great advice for any business owners reading this. James Sinclair, thank you very much for joining us.

Thank you.

Three Key Lessons
From James Sinclair

1. **Turn your Fast Pounds into Slow Pounds** – your salary or income can leave your bank account as quickly as it arrives, so you need to learn to live on 50% of your income and invest the rest in assets such as property that throw off Slow Pounds. Use the slow pounds to pay for the fancy cars and holidays.

2. **Buy the premises you run your business from** – not only does this give you an appreciating asset, it puts you in control of one of your business's biggest overheads – the rent. (*I actually own the building my business trades from in my pension plan so my company is paying rent into my pension every month – GR*)

3. **Hire employees so you can do the important stuff!** Most business owners try to leave it as long as possible before hiring staff. This is a mistake because you need to think like an Entrepreneur and appoint managers to operate the business. You lead and set the vision, they tidy up the mess and make your vision a reality!

Marquess of Bristol

Marquess of Bristol
From Eton to Estonia

Frederick Hervey, 8th Marquess of Bristol succeeded his elder half-brother the 7th Marquess (1954–1999) in January 1999 as Marquess of Bristol. He is also the 12th Earl of Bristol, Earl Jermyn of Horningsheath in the County of Suffolk, 13th Baron Hervey of Ickworth in the County of Suffolk, and Hereditary High Steward of the Liberty of St Edmund, which encompasses the whole former county of West Suffolk.

The 8th Marquess is the only son of the late 6th Marquess by his third wife, the former Yvonne Sutton. He is the brother of Lady Victoria Hervey and Lady Isabella Hervey.

He was educated at St Maur School in Monaco, Sunningdale School, Eton College, and the University of Edinburgh, from which he graduated with a Bachelor of Commerce degree

After leaving university in 2002, he moved to Estonia, where he lived for seven years and managed a Baltic property fund. He is currently the CEO and founder of property investment platform Brickowner - see more at Brickowner.com

On 11 May 2018 Lord Bristol married Meredith Dunn, an American art consultant.

My guest in this chapter is someone whose family history goes back hundreds of years, but he's recently started disrupting the property market with his new business. He is Frederick the 8th Marquess of Bristol. Frederick, welcome to Money & Me.

Thank you very much for having me Graham.

I believe your early years were spent growing up in Monaco, which I know well - I'm in the slightly less tax efficient end of the Côte d'Azur in Antibes myself - but tell me what it was like growing up and going to school in that part of the world?

Yes, actually there were a lot of British people there at the time, quite a lot of Italians, it wasn't as flashy as you would get now, but amazing weather and a really lovely environment when you're a child to be brought up in, for all the right reasons in the sense it's just a very friendly, safe place to be brought up.

And I guess you became fluent in French?

Exactly, so I went to school there when I was very young as well and obviously when you're a child, children pick up languages much faster than adults.

Absolutely, I wish I had done it at that age. But then you end up in Eton, which obviously is famous for producing a lot of Cabinet Ministers, but did you learn much there that was helpful from a finance or an investing or a business point of view?

Yes, I think Eton is amazing in the way that they teach you what they believe a young man needs to know, not what the government who happen to be in power believes should be the national curriculum. So a lot of what they teach you is not even on the curriculum but they believe you need to know it. For example the history goes all the way from ancient history all the way to the present, whereas the curriculum is focused only on modern history. I think it's a really great school actually, so I had very good years there and I'm very appreciative of going there as well.

One of my pet complaints is that the education system doesn't really cover things like finance and investing, did they touch on any of that kind of stuff at Eton or was money even a topic of discussion?

I think in a good way they've got amazing facilities but I personally have always been quite mathematical, maths was one of my A-Levels along with economics and French, so I was always interested in the more financial and numerical aspects of education.

What were your early thoughts about what you might do as a career after leaving university?

I was at Edinburgh University, I did a four year course because all of the courses at Edinburgh are four years. Each summer I did a different internship, one at a bank which I hated, one at a stock broking firm which I also hated, and then between my third and fourth year I spent a month in Eastern Europe in Estonia and I really loved it and that was in 2001.

Okay, well we'll come back to that in a moment, but while you were at university that's when there were two family tragedies that led to you going very quickly from third in line for inheriting the title of Marquess to actually being the Marquess. You lost two members of the family in little over a year, that's must have been a very traumatic time?

Yes though it's a long time ago, it's 20 years ago now, so I think in a funny way, when you're young, at that age ironically I think you're probably better at coping or adapting. I think humans are very versatile, it's amazing, if you look at history, even the wars people have been through and they come out as emotionally healthy people. At the time obviously it wasn't easy but I think I have come through it as a well-adjusted person.

Okay, but if you think about it albeit on a slightly different scale perhaps, George VI inherited the throne from Edward and felt unprepared for it, you were a very young man and then suddenly you inherited the title, was there a sense of 'gosh what am I going to do with this now?'

Not really because I was already on my own path and I'm a very individual person, meaning I've always done what I want to do, not in a selfish way but in a healthy way.

So it didn't really affect my path. It was probably the reason why I ended up moving abroad because in a good way it's out of the rat race, you can become more of your own person without everyone staring at you.

Okay, let's talk about that move abroad. You were saying you'd spent time in Estonia in one of your assignments at university and then suddenly you end up going to live and work there and get involved in I think a Baltic property fund?

Exactly.

Tell me about how that all came about.

When I did my work experience in 2001, it was pre-EU, so we were looking at some properties, for which you could get pre-accession grants. I thought I had a job lined up when I left university, so I left in June 2002 and I moved there in September and then I quickly found that the job I thought I had wasn't there. So I ended up straight away doing my own thing because either I do that or I come back to England. I was 21, so I thought I might as well just stick it out.

And I started off with some agency brokering and then, which you'll like actually, some of the islands there were being privatised. But only the residents had the ability to privatise, they didn't have the money, so you could back-to-back the contracts so you would in effect buy it off them before they even owned it and at a big discount because they would get a 50% discount to market and we would buy it off them at a 30% discount, so straight away they're making 20% out of thin air.

So I started doing that. And then from that I met Toby, who also works with me now actually, and he was working for the Soros Foundation in South East Europe, and from there we started working more with the investors and doing some of our own deals as well.

So you effectively created your own fund and you looked for these kind of property investment opportunities in those Baltic countries?

Yes so technically we had a mandate for any of the Baltic states, Latvia, Lithuania, Estonia; they're all pretty different, they're all tiny really, especially Estonia, but we only invested in Estonia and because it's such a small country in a great way it was a very broad spectrum value added investments. So if we bought an office building it was because it had a car park at the back where you could build out extra square feet. So yes it was an interesting learning curve.

Well even today Estonia is cited as one of the emerging economies where there's huge opportunity, so I guess you were in ahead of that curve. You must have felt that you could do anything there because you were so early into the game.

Yes and they're a very young country demographically – I was young at the time as well, so were the people in power - even the Prime Minister was in his 30s. You weren't looked down upon because of being a younger age either. And it was very dynamic. Even then I think they had E-voting, they've always been very much into their tech as such.

So what was it that brought you back from Estonia and the Baltics to work back in Britain on the family estates?

It wasn't a conscious decision, it was more of a pull. I just suddenly had more and more things that were taking my time, which were in the UK. In the early days in Estonia, I might have only come back to the UK for say four days every seven weeks. But, as you grow older, you want to see your friends and your family more, so I tied that in with work. And I started looking at different properties in East Anglia and the Midlands, Lincolnshire in particular and investing there as well.

So how were you able to use what you'd learned in the Baltics when you came back to this country? Did you feel then that you had that confidence and experience of how to spot a good property development opportunity regardless of what country it was in?

Yes, with Estonia not having been an independent country for very long, people are often more creative or entrepreneurial. It's an interesting way of thinking. So I think maybe I learned some of that and to spot opportunities where maybe some other people can't. I guess looking at things differently to other people is always good.

Before we come on to your ground-breaking disruptive work in the property industry, what would you say were the main lessons you learned from those first years both in the Baltics and in this country about property investment?

That you can research and do structured education for decades but actually it is completely different to practical learning! It's all about practical learning - that's what I found very quickly. Because everything is about people, interaction, reading people, understanding people's motivations, a lot like psychology. So I guess that's the main thing that I was learning, especially in Estonia and I'm very interested in people anyway and what makes them tick.

So Frederick, tell me a little bit about the transition from running these property developments in East Anglia and Lincolnshire and then somehow the germ of this idea to do something with a property platform comes to you. How did that actually come about?

It didn't happen by accident but I wasn't trying to think of something new to set up. I was actually in a particular area in Lincolnshire looking at buying up new houses. You could buy them for below new build costs and there was a strong rental demand, so I thought this is really interesting. I was talking to Toby, who I used to work with a long time ago in Estonia, saying I really want to look at setting up a property fund to do this. He said don't do that, set up a platform, because for the last five years he'd been living in Berlin and he was running a technology accelerator. So he was quite ingrained in that whole tech world. I thought this looked really interesting and he said that by automating all the processes of know your clients, anti-money laundering and onboarding, the costs incrementally decrease so suddenly you can scale much quicker, more smoothly and you can technically take smaller amounts of money for investments and aggregate them.

That was in early 2015, so it got the seed going and then over the course of that summer I started writing the business plan and honing it and changing it and then we started building the platform. It took a year to build the platform; all of 2016 was building the platform, ten people full time, all they were doing was building the technology.

Right, because I think these days the fashionable expression is a minimum viable product, so was this to get you going, you had to get at least a certain amount of core functionality?

Yes so when they talk about minimum viable product, what a lot of people do which is bad, is you 'over-build' the products because you think you know who your clients or your user will be and you cater too much to them an then you're wrong! So for us it was all about the minimum viable product had to be an investment platform where people can invest easily without too many bells and whistles, so that's in effect that we launched in late January 2017. We launched the platform and from there we've carried on growing.

I suppose in a sense you then had the same dilemma that I live with on a daily basis, which is that you need investors and you need stuff for them to invest in and you've got to try and find them both at the same time, so how did you go about that?

Firstly it helps that all I've ever done is property, so I know a lot of people in the property world who work with investors. That was really where we found the first few deals and partners and that hasn't really changed. And what's often happened is some of those people have then become shareholders, so we've even done deals where some of the property asset managers then become some of our shareholders and in a good way you kind of grow together.

Right.

In terms of the investor base, again we have a lot of shareholders, that helps. It's all about trust so it's a question of trying to break down the trust barriers so people trust you more and you grow from there. I always talk about the analogy of a dartboard, so the centre would be people who are friends and family who we know or who we work with, that's kind of the ultimate trust and as you go out, each circle represents slightly less trust, so you've got to cater for each circle one at a time.

This is where I do struggle a bit with the platform concept because you were saying earlier about the biggest thing you'd learned in property investment was it was all about the people, and yet in a sense a platform can come across as somewhat impersonal. And I'm not sure if it's a generational thing - I mainly deal with people in their mid-40s to mid-60s who seem to like to get to know people first before they make an investment - whereas perhaps the younger generation who are brought up with this technology are very comfortable just to go on their phone and start making investments?

Yes, I think it's a balance. I think one of the important things that no one wants to interact with is all the paperwork in relation to making investments. No one wants to be given 100 pages of documents, you have to get your bank statements certified, your passport certified. No one wants that so we take all of that hassle away, it's all automated. So that is an amazing thing about our platform.

In terms of the personal thing, I agree with you, so we're always at the end of the phone and people can call us. And we're always online where we have a pop-up, you can ask questions online instantly, so there's always a real person, its not a bot, a real person answering that. What we're doing is making it more flexible so maybe if someone is at work and can't spend 20 minutes on the phone talking to us, they can just ask the odd question, go back to doing something at work, then come back ten minutes later and have an answer. So it's about flexibility and I think and that's what we provide.

And I guess the flexibility extends to things like the amount available to invest because typically these property projects are fairly capital intensive and what you're doing now is opening it up to people who might only have a few hundred or a few thousand to invest rather than six or seven figures?

That's true but we actually have a low minimum of £100 but what we've found, and what most of the other platforms have found, is they end up with an average of £20,000 per person. The low minimum is really just about trust. So people might test the platform with £100, transfer it in, invest it, they get their first dividend, oh, and then transfer £10,000 or £15,000 or £20,000 or £50,000 into an investment. So really it's about building that trust.

Also some people like to drip feed their investments in, so the low minimum is all about flexibility and trust.

I think also what I've found useful is where it becomes a kind of an adjunct to an existing relationship, so for example we develop relationships with people over a number of years and then when we say we can take the pain away of dealing with lawyers by giving you access to this platform, the combination of the two seems to have worked really well.

I agree with you, and I think in my mind it's the future. And people's lives now, they're very demanding, people travel a lot, people want to be able to invest 24/7 when it suits them not when their stockbroker is in or the banks are open. It's ridiculous, they're open between 10 and 4 o'clock, and they're probably away for an hour for lunch so it's crazy.

Two of the questions I always try and ask are what else and what next. You got the platform up and running in 2017, and it's obviously expanding its range of projects and so on, what else have you got planned for where you're going to take the platform?

We're going to launch a secondary market so people can sell. At the moment they can invest in an automated way. But we're also going to create a marketplace where people can sell. As you know, obviously property is illiquid, so people can't always get out when they necessarily want to if they want to get out early. So we're going to create the ability to enable them to get out early. And also we've applied to be directly authorised so we'll be able to create our own ISA products, we'll create auto invest functionality and just add on more and more products and cater to our users because they tell us what they want.

And I guess this would be an innovative finance type ISA would it?

Exactly yes.

So I could make an investment in property but have the returns in a tax-free wrapper?

Exactly yes.

And obviously it becomes a lot more attractive doesn't it.

Yes!

Okay, so that's in the future, is there a grand plan for the longer-term future for you and your family? What would you like to see happen over the coming years and decades?

Well as you say, I've just got married recently so touch wood at some point we'll have some children, hopefully happy, well-adjusted children, and I guess it's like anything, it's about balance. I think the three main bits in any person's life are work, friends and family and it's a question of getting the balance between all three of them.

Right okay. So you came into the title of Marquess in fairly tragic circumstances, you've now had 20 years to adjust to that, you've got your business where you want it, what do you want the legacy to be that you will leave to the 9th Marquess?

I think for me, it's interesting that success in anything, not just financial stuff, any type of success is a bi-product of doing something you're, by default, good at. Which probably means you have to enjoy it to be good at it. So I think for me, it's important that I'd want them to be open-minded and just not feel they have to do anything or go in this or that direction. To be able to do whatever makes them fulfilled as people. And I think, by default, if they do that, if anyone does that, I think you become successful.

And will some kind of teaching or passing on of wisdom in the areas of money and investing be part of the upbringing for those kids?

Yes, obviously I like property, I like real investments, I like things I can understand that are tangible and for me anyone should like all of those as well. And I think, especially with children, it's getting the balance right in giving them access to enough. So they've got a roof over their head but not giving them too much so it stunts creativity or creates laziness. To be frank, I wouldn't want that either.

Okay so I guess no regrets about that decision not to become a banker?

Definitely not, no!

Frederick, Marquess of Bristol, thanks very much for joining us.

Thanks a lot Graham.

Three Key Lessons
From the Marquess of Bristol

1. **The best opportunities may be overseas** – Frederick discovered Estonia by accident and found enormous opportunity there. The skills and experience he acquired in that young, developing country have helped him think differently to many UK property developers.

2. **Use technology to solve people's problems** – investment involves a lot of paperwork which the Brickowner platform automates. By bringing these costs down the platform is able to allow minimum investments as low as £100 which opens up property investing to a wider audience.

3. **Trust and flexibility are key to customer relationships** – you need to find ways to help people increase their trust in you, for example by offering a low minimum investment to test a new platform, and you need to be flexible so that you fit into people's busy lives in a way that is convenient for them. You just have to look at the growth in online shopping to see how important flexibility and convenience have become.

Luke Lang

Luke Lang
Democratising Equity Investment

Before co-founding Crowdcube in 2011, Luke held specialist marketing roles in companies ranging from start-up firms to FTSE 100 brands, and also his own consultancy. As co-founder and Chief Marketing Officer of Crowdcube, the world's largest equity investment crowdfunding platform, he regularly provides comment to the global media on entrepreneurship, business finance and personal investment.

He was named by Debrett's as one of Britain's 500 most influential people in 2017, and was also selected as one of the Sunday Times 'Maserati 100' game-changing entrepreneurs. He is an active investor and a keen cyclist.

My guest today is the co-founder of Crowdcube, the world's largest crowd funding platform, and he's been nominated as one of the 500 most influential people in the country and was named by the Sunday Times as one of the top 100 movers and shakers in the world of entrepreneurs; his name is Luke Lang. Luke welcome to Money & Me.

Pleased to be here.

Okay, let's take you back a little bit to your childhood growing up before you got into business. I think your father was a carpenter and a builder and it seems like quite an entrepreneurial family because you and several of your siblings have ended up with your own businesses?

Yes, I'm not sure either my mum or my dad would have ever considered themselves as entrepreneurs, but looking back, in hindsight, they definitely displayed entrepreneurial traits - that drive, determination, bravery, looking for opportunities. My dad was a carpenter but he started several successful businesses. My mum worked in education but was very much a pioneer of vocational learning and apprenticeships at a time when apprenticeships were at their lowest level in the late 1980s/early 1990s, and really drove a revolution in and around Devon and made that into a thing that ended up getting folded into the local college.

So yes I don't think they would ever consider themselves as entrepreneurial but it certainly rubbed off. My eldest brother Mark saw the opportunity in the internet and when dial up and broadband internet was coming - so he set up a company that I worked for, that's where I was really blooded in the world of entrepreneurialism and start-up culture. My sister and her husband run a successful housing company and my other brother is an engineer and I myself am at Crowdcube. So yes, there's very much an entrepreneurial gene in the family for sure.

So you joined your brother's business and was it a case of learning your trade there before deciding to go out on your own with your own company?

Yes very much, I was fortunate, Mark started Eclipse Internet around when dial up was just starting and really I joined just as we were riding the wave of broadband penetration into the mainstream. And it was a really exciting place to work, it was really innovative, lots of product development, it was fast-paced, it was very, very competitive. So there were lots of synergies between Eclipse Internet and my company, Crowdcube, and I took a lot of learning from that and brought that across to my company as well.

To be fair, from my own experience, learning is one thing but I think until you've done it nothing prepares you for the culture shock of actually going out on your own and being in business for yourself and having to make all the decisions and having to do everything and wearing so many hats. How did you find that transition?

Well I was fortunate enough to have a partner in Darren, so we co-founded the company back in 2010. And I think that helps hugely, you know you've got a sounding board, you share the successes and celebrate the successes but also you share the burden and the stress and the strain as well. And I think you need to be a particular type of person - entrepreneurs are brave, they're courageous, they're determined and I think if you don't have those traits its very difficult to succeed, certainly in the early stages of starting a business, where those characteristics are really, really important.

And also I think if you look at timing, because in a sense you started Crowdcube at a time when we were just coming out of the worst financial crisis since the 1920s. So you might have thought that's not ideal timing...

Absolutely yes and most people that I met said exactly that. You know we started thinking about Crowdcube back in 2007/2008 right around the time that the economic crash was happening and we launched in 2011. A lot of people that I spoke to said this is insane, well-known companies on the high street are going bust let alone businesses that you hadn't heard of, so the idea that entrepreneurs would put their business plan onto our website and then invite investors to back and support them was an alien concept. People were very guarded in those early days, thinking 'I don't want to share my business plan because my competitors will be able to steal what I do'.

And equally, you were seeing investors whose investments were depreciating, we'd had the worst economic crash since the 1920s, so the very notion that they would be backing and investing in high risk start-up early stage businesses was also quite alien to a lot of people. But you know we firmly believed in what we were doing and we saw the success of Kickstarter in the US where the notion and the principles behind crowd funding were really taking hold. There was proof of concept there, and for us equity crowd funding was just an extension of reward-based crowd funding. You're not backing a business or a person or a product and getting a T-shirt, you're backing and getting an equity stake in that business, so you're owning a piece of it. And still today that is very much an evolutionary step in crowd funding.

Well I'd go further, I'd say you've been at the epicentre of what I can only call an entrepreneurial revolution, because if I go back perhaps even just a generation, I don't think Brits were that entrepreneurial, so what do you think has changed?

I don't know; we're allegedly a nation of shopkeepers so I think there was always an entrepreneurial gene within the British public. I guess we helped to fuel that entrepreneurship and specifically, the businesses that we helped to fund, they're very ambitious, they're bright, they're determined, they're earlier stage, increasingly later stage actually, a lot of the companies are raising in excess of £5 million on the site now.

So we are very much helping to fuel that generation. In 2017, one in four entrepreneurs in the UK that raised equity finance did it on a crowd funding platform. There was research by Ernst & Young just before Christmas that said entrepreneurs' second preference, after venture capital investment, was crowd funding and we actually outranked bank finance for the first time.

And what I think is interesting, there are two sides to this story, there are the entrepreneurs themselves who are driven to set up a business and take all those risks that we're talking about, but then there's all these people that are willing to invest in them, because you can't have one without the other.

Yes and that's one of the things that I'm most proud of, that we've democratised investment, we've made investing that prior to Crowdcube was restricted to the wealthy and the well connected available to everyone. Everyday people who can back and invest in a business from as little as £10, happily they invest a lot more than that, we've had individuals who invest up to £1 million on the platform, the average investment is around about £1,500 to £2,000 so they are significant sums of money.

And people are building portfolios as well. One of the things that we stress is we don't shy away from the fact that investing in early stage businesses is high risk and we make no bones about that, but we're very clear about the notion that you should be thinking about diversifying, you should be thinking about building a portfolio in the same way that you would build a portfolio of stocks and shares in your ISA or your pension. Equity investment is the interesting, exciting part of your portfolio that maybe only takes up 10-15% of your net investible assets. But maybe it's the stuff that's a bit more exciting and you're allowed to unleash some of your passions and get a sense of some of the impact that you're making with your investment, whether it be job creation in the local area, whether it be economic impact, whether it be environmental or social impact.

Okay, well I think that's an important point that you talk about there because, although it's very easy to make the investments on a platform like that, you're actually starting a fairly long journey because most of these companies are going to take several years to grow to the point where you might get an exit. And people I think have to be very cognisant of that.

Yes absolutely, that's one of the risks, they are long term investments and you're investing early. The upsides are great, if that business goes on to become a unicorn, and we're very privileged to have had the likes of Monzo, the challenger bank Revolut, BrewDog the craft brewer have all raised on our platform and have gone on to become billion dollar plus companies. Not all of them will - lots of them won't be as successful as that, many will fail, but typically it's a long term play, you're investing five to ten years typically before you get a return.

And I guess the answer is that you have to become a miniature venture capitalist and have a little portfolio of seven, eight, nine, ten companies?

Yes absolutely, we've got people with portfolios spread across hundreds of businesses.

Typically it's around five to ten but that's growing all the time as the repeat investment rate is high. So that message is certainly sinking in that you don't just invest in one business, you look to spread that money around and spread that risk around and potentially you get a return.

So Luke, if we go back to childhood days, were you taught sort of disciplines of saving and investing and financial literacy by your parents?

So I think one of the things that really stands out for me in my childhood was that getting a bank account for the first time was a big deal, and I got a bank account with NatWest and I was one of that generation that saved up and got the NatWest pigs. I was very much driven and focused on saving that £100 so I could get the full collection. Even though I think this is hotly disputed; the five pigs still at my father's house, my sister still contests who actually owns all five. So I'm not quite sure how that's going to pan out.

Let's talk now about one of the sectors that's really benefited from this sort of crowd funding and that's financial technology or FinTech.

When you talk about FinTech, one of the things that I see is how it's taking a very simplistic model and digitising that and teaching people about financial planning, about saving and about financial inclusion as well. You're right, FinTech has benefitted hugely, more than any other sector, from crowd funding, from equity finance. We've had businesses like the challenger bank, Monzo, just a few months ago they raised £20 million through crowd funding working with us. We've had Revolut, another unicorn business, companies like goHenry, which is all about credit cards for kids and teaching children financial literacy. They learn how to manage their money and the platform gives parents the opportunity to track and understand how the kids are spending their money and when they're spending it and linking it to their chores and to things like that.

Which I remember as a child growing up, money was very much valued, we were taught the value of money and we weren't just given it, you had to work for it. In a family of six, there were plenty of school shirts to iron and after that there were plenty of cars to wash on the drive to earn my pocket money.

Companies like goHenry are digitising that; they're bringing it into the 21st century. Chip is another great example of a company that, using artificial intelligence (AI), monitors your current account and then works out how you can save money without ever really noticing that you are.

So there are lots of businesses that I think have a real deep sense of purpose and they're making a difference, whether it be through changing people's behaviour, increasing and improving financial literacy or improving inclusion. And I think they see the benefit of crowd funding.

My view is that the new breed of financial services technologies company understands that there is a lot of discontent and dissatisfaction with traditional banks and finance and they understand that using crowd funding and enabling their customers and their community to invest and back them using crowd funding, is a way of differentiating themselves. It's a way of saying we're different, we're not like the old guard, we want you to be involved, we want you to be on this journey with us and to create a new financial services sector that everyone can be proud of.

Well certainly if ever a sector deserved disruption I think it's the High Street banks, so I would say amen to all of that. And also I think what we can do there is use something very close to younger people's hearts, which is their phones and the related technology to achieve something that the core education system has singularly failed to achieve, which is some degree of financial literacy.

Yes absolutely, and I think I would go one step further, financial literacy should be on the curriculum, we should be teaching it from a very early age. There's evidence to suggest that you learn your financial habits, whether saving or spending, very, very early on in your life.

Yes, that's true.

So I think teaching people at a young age would be hugely beneficial for the country. And finances, whether you're in debt or whether you're able to save, is linked to mental health as well, so there are huge benefits not just in financial services but for the NHS in that if you can get people managing their finances better, it makes you feel better, it means that you're less likely to suffer from mental illness.

These companies are trying to solve some of those challenges, trying to help people manage their finances much better.

Okay, so moving away from crowd funding for a moment, do you have time to invest in other things, are there any other areas that you actually invest in personally outside the core business?

In terms of financial investments?

Yes.

Yes I'm probably typical of a lot of entrepreneurs, where you're focused so intently on the business and growing it that you maybe sacrifice your own personal financial planning. So I've got a pension but it's pretty pitiful; I'm trying to sort that out now. And I have started doing some ISAs, I use Nutmeg for my ISAs, another FinTech business that's made huge growth in the last five years, so trying to maximise those tax allowances that you get there and of course the investments that I do through Crowdcube as well.

Okay, and away from the business and investing world, you're quite into your fitness, I think you did something rather special for your 40th birthday last year?

Yes I did, I did a leg of the Tour de France, out from Lake Annecy over four mountains, 4,000 metres of climbing over 100 miles or so. So yes I love being on my bike, when I'm not at work or spending time with my partner and my children, I love nothing more than being on the bike and flying up and down mountains.

And the odd triathlon as well I think?

Yes so I pushed myself a little bit further and taught myself to swim and forced myself to run, know those are the two bits really that sandwich the cycling bit that I kind of endure. But I like the challenge, I like setting myself targets and goals and stretching myself, so cycling and triathlons and I did a half Ironman a few years ago, which was probably one of my greater achievements on a bike.

Okay, now let's assume we're moving into a parallel universe here and you'd set up a political career, we're obviously going through the whole Brexit thing at the moment, what would you do if you were running the country to try and make things better from a business, or an entrepreneurial or an investing perspective?

I think there are a lot of great tax incentives out there and a lot of great initiatives and a lot of great policies that successive governments have put in place.

You know I remember the privatisation of BT, I remember my dad buying shares on my behalf and as a child in the 1980s - I used to religiously look at the paper every day and track those shares. Though I don't know that I quite knew what it all meant.

I think there have been a number of initiatives over the years. I feel like we need to educate people better and that needs to start much earlier on, so as I said earlier I think it needs to form part of the curriculum much earlier on.

And I think there's more that the government can do to stimulate start-up early stage businesses. Traditionally we were a nation of shopkeepers, now I think we're a nation of entrepreneurs as well, so the more that we can do to nurture that and nurture particular sectors the better. We've spoken about financial services and FinTech, we genuinely lead the world on some of these things and I think the government could do more to shine a spotlight on that.

You talk to a lot of entrepreneurs obviously, what do you hear are some of their challenges that maybe the politicians could help with?

I think hiring and recruitment and talent is always a big challenge for businesses, particularly tech businesses, whether you're a FinTech or whether you're educational technology or its agricultural technology or clean tech; getting access to the engineering talent to be able to build that technology is quite tough and keeping hold of it can be quite tough.

And sometimes you have big companies like Google that come in and put their European Headquarters in the centre of London at King's Cross and everyone thinks that's an amazing thing. It is and it's something that we should be proud of, but that does suck talent from those start-up early stage businesses because of people that want to go and work at Google for instance. So it's about striking the right balance there.

Okay. And what are the characteristics that you see of the people that seem to be the most successful entrepreneurs - you see so many of them, what are the top two or three things that you think you've got to have if you're going to be a successful entrepreneur?

Well first and foremost you need to have a great idea; a good product, a good service and you need to have a clearly identifiable market and opportunity. I see a trend towards businesses being not just successful at raising finance, but to be successful more generally you need a really clear purpose about why you are there.

For example BrewDog is not just a brewery, they're on a mission to make craft brewery amazing. Monzo is not just another bank; they're on a mission to have a community-created bank and to challenge the status quo.

So I think businesses with a clear purpose and vision and mission of what they want to do and how they want to solve real problems are the most successful. I think people identify with those problems and that makes these companies successful.

And for the entrepreneurs themselves, it's a bit of a cliché but that kind of drive, determination, that visionary, really strong leadership is what sets them apart. I think all entrepreneurs are brave, you need to have courage because you take a lot of risks and I think sometimes people are afraid of failing. I view failures as just stepping stones on the way to finding the right answer and to success. So you need to embrace that fear of failure or making mistakes.

Finally Luke, what's next for Crowdcube? You've got to the point now where you're probably the biggest platform of your type in the world, where do you want to go with it next?

Yes, there's still a lot to do with it in the UK. As I said, one in four entrepreneurs that raised equity finance did it through crowd funding, but I think there's still a huge amount of growth there. We've seen growth in the regions - crowd funding was pioneered in London and now, as it's maturing, it's really starting to get out into the regions and we're seeing more companies from around the British Isles raising finance on Crowdcube and attracting more investors from the region as well so growing that for sure.

We've also seen growth from Europe as well, so we've got offices in Barcelona and we've seen growth in European businesses looking to raise finance on our platform. So certainly we will be consolidating our position in the UK and growing it, but also we'll be looking at further expansion in Europe and beyond.

And is there any potential scope for, a bit of a coals to Newcastle story, but would you be tempted to go into the American market?

We've got a relationship with the leading crowd funding platform in the US, a strategic partnership that enables us to put some of our businesses on their platform to raise finance in the US and for some US firms to raise finance over here. So that's a really good way of us starting to really understand that market and give our investors and our entrepreneurs exposure to it as well.

And, from what I'm seeing, some of the most exciting emerging economies are now over in Asia, have you got any plans to go East as well?

Not right now, no, I think we've got our plate full with the UK, Europe and the US, but it's certainly something that we would explore. Also the Indian and Chinese markets have a huge entrepreneurial scene so yes there's certainly opportunity.

So if anyone's reading this thinking is now the time for me to get involved in investing in start ups, what would you response to that be?

I would say go online, do your research, look at the platforms that are out there, look at the investments that are out there. You don't need to rush in, you can invest from as little as £10 so you can dip your toe in to begin with and then build from there. And certainly if you're looking at making an investment do your due diligence, look into the business, read the forums, try and understand the market, the opportunity and the people behind the company and try and make a really informed decision.

Brilliant okay. Luke Lang, thank you very much.

Thank you very much.

Three Key Lessons
From Luke Lang

1. **Do your own due diligence!** Investing in early stage companies is both risky and long term. Make sure you understand what they do, how they make money and how credible their business plan is. Who are their competitors and what differentiates the company you are looking to invest in?

2. **Become a mini Venture Capitalist** – spread your investment across at least 5, preferably 10 companies to increase your chances of at least one being a huge success. A typical VC will expect 3 or 4 companies to fail, 3 or 4 to just about wash their face and 1 or 2 to be successful. Their success should more than cover the cost of the other investments and might just make you a fortune if you discover a unicorn.

3. **Don't Suffer Cobblers Shoes syndrome** – like many entrepreneurs, Luke is totally focussed on his own business and has very few assets outside it. You need to learn that your business exists for one sole purpose – so that you can take money out of it! Read the James Sinclair interview on fast pounds and slow pounds for more on this.

Section 3

The Writers

Claer Barrett

Dominic Frisby

John Stepek

Claer Barrett

Claer Barrett

De-mystifying Money for the Masses

Claer is one of the UK's leading financial journalists, a recent winner of the Financial Journalist of the Year Award. Her aim is to demystify money matters to help people make the most of their finances. An experienced broadcaster, she frequently appears on radio and TV and speaks at finance related events.

She is the FT's Personal Finance Editor and writes a weekly column, Serious Money, in the FT Money section of the Weekend FT. She also presents a daily business and finance bulletin on Eddie Mair's Drive show on LCB radio just after 5.30pm Monday to Friday where she talks about the three biggest business and finance stories of the day. She also presents the weekly FT Money Show podcast.

Learn more about Claer at the Financial Times website ft.com

In this chapter my guest is one of the UK's top financial journalists and the winner of the Financial Commentator of the Year Award, Claer Barrett. Claer, welcome to Money & Me.

Thanks for having me Graham.

Now we have a female Dr Who now so I think I'm in my rights to ask you to take us in your TARDIS back to your childhood and just tell me a little bit about the kind of family environment you grew up in and whether money was ever a topic of conversation with your parents.

More a way of life I would say than a topic of conversation. I mean I grew up in the late 70s/early 80s and back then, unlike now, only one parent worked, my dad, and my mum gave up work to raise me and my brother. And my mum and dad both work as teachers, so they didn't have very much money, neither of their families had very much money and my goodness; we knew that we didn't have much money. But it wasn't ever portrayed to us in a bad light or a negative light.

Sure there were friends of mine at school, especially when I got older and became a teenager, who had say Nike Air trainers. I can remember when they first came out and my dad saying '£45 for a pair of trainers!'. So there was no way I was ever going to get a pair of trainers because that wasn't something that they placed any value on.

However, they did buy me a saxophone when I was 13 which cost £600 and that involved many years of saving up and help from grandma, but until I had an accident and nearly knocked one of my teeth out when I was a bit older, that was what I was going to do for a career - I was intent on becoming a professional musician. And so it's a bit like the John Lewis advert now with the child, Elton John, being given a piano by his grandparents.

They were very focused on spending money on the right things and they still are and I still am now and I'm lucky enough to earn now, in terms of my annual salary and pension and everything, way in excess of what either of my parents ever earned in their lifetime. They're both now retired, but I am still as stingy as hell.

So they drummed that into you from early doors?

Oh yes, and in particular, they're both really good at it, but my dad is really good at it and we text each other all the time saying 'ooh Marks & Spark's points promotions' or this is happening or there's a very good offer on wine in a particular supermarket. Because he's retired now so he's got a lot more time to search out the best ways of spending his money. But it was always made into a fun thing.

I can remember we used to drive in the 1980s a mile away to a farm that sold trays of cracked eggs. You wouldn't be able to legally sell or eat them now in the post-salmonella era, but it was a great adventure, off we'd go off to the farm in our wellies and go and buy a tray of cracked eggs for 20p or something ridiculous.

So they were very frugal my parents, but they made saving money fun.

Okay, so at what point does a saxophone give way to the typewriter and you become a journalist?

Well when I was at school – you probably won't believe this – I was actually incredibly shy and when I went to secondary school it was almost the worst thing that ever happened to me because I was surrounded by all of these children that I didn't know, there were hardly any people from my school that had gone to this school. And so for the first couple of years it was just all about survival and staying out of the way of the big girls in the year above, who used to come across to me as being particularly frightening.

Anyway, one day at school I was wearing my Dr Martens boots, which are still fashionable now but then especially, at the age of 13 I had my first pair of Dr Martens, which I saved up for ages to get. And one of the teachers came up to me and said 'oh Barrett, I don't think girls should be allowed to wear these boots because they don't look very feminine' and I said, 'well they're a lot better for your feet sir than wearing high heels', which some of my contemporaries were already wearing at that stage. Anyway this went further and the school decided to ban girls from wearing Dr Marten boots.

And this is basically what transformed me from a shy and retiring person, who wouldn't really like to even speak in class for fear of making an idiot of herself, to becoming a warrior for justice in the campaign for girls to wear DMs!

And I got up a petition; I phoned up the local paper, I was queuing up every morning outside the staff room to tell the teachers what was happening. I became the most popular person in the school practically overnight because everyone wore DMs, it wasn't just me, and everyone just got behind this campaign.

And we won and they overturned it and said this is ridiculous. Some of the female teachers especially got behind it and said, you can't tell girls that wearing DMs with a skirt is unfeminine – I still wear DMs now and I suspect I will do for some time to come.

But that was what it took to make me think 'oh I'm so angry about this, I'm going to fight for it to be changed and overcome my shyness'.

And I think for me that's what a lot of really good journalism is all about, it's about noticing and shining a light on something that isn't fair. And unfortunately, within the world of finance and particularly personal finance, there is an awful lot of stuff that falls under that category and trying to change something, bring it into the public interest and do some good.

Excellent, then you went to university?

Eventually, I worked for two years before I went to university, I didn't want to go to university.

Ah, but eventually you succumbed because you also did a Master's Degree.

I did yes.

Then you ended up going into property journalism initially after graduating, is that correct?

Yes, that's right, because at that time I was still trying to make it as a musician you see, so I wasn't interested in academia and I decided okay, I will go to university but I'll go in London because that's where all the bands are, and then I joined the university newspaper and that was kind of it. So I thought writing was OK, but I still didn't think I'd be any good at it and so I thought I'll stick to working as a secretary because that's what I was doing for my 'good job', to get out of debt, and you could make very good money being a secretary and there were lots of jobs.

And the temping agency, in fact just round the corner from this skyscraper, the very insightful person who booked me said, 'what do you actually want to do for a career now that you've finished your degree?' and I said 'well I want to be a journalist but you're not going to get me a job as that', and she said 'well I can get you secretary to the editor of a trade magazine'. So the next day I started there and within three months I'd got on the graduate trainee scheme and that was it.

Oh wow, that was serendipitous. So you already wanted to be a journalist, you just didn't think you had an avenue into it and then you got there through a secretarial role and then managed to impress them with your writing skills?

Or because of my organisation skills; you know I think to be a journalist you need to be really, really well organised, and you need to be good at running your own personal finances; it's also a key skill.

One of the reasons that I am so organised is because I had a really horrible experience when I was 17, and I got the day wrong for one of my A-Levels. I wasn't particularly careful in those days about things like whether it was a Tuesday or a Thursday, and I can remember, I was at home, I'd just got out of bed and Mr Goth phoned up from school and said, 'Barrett why aren't you here?' and I was thinking, 'well because my exam's on Thursday', and he said, 'no its just started'. And I managed to knock on all the neighbours' doors and get one of them to take me to the school.

I hadn't really done the right revision because I'd left all of that to the last minute as well. And they let me into the exam, which was very kind of them – I'm sure they bent the rules – and I still passed. So I had done enough, but it could easily have gone the other way and that was the most important exam of all of the A-Levels that I was taking.

So that got you organised?

I felt wretched for the whole rest of the summer waiting for those results, and I just thought I never ever want anything like this to happen to me ever again. So it was the kick in the bum that I needed to actually grow up and say, I have to be responsible for my own destiny.

But to go back to being a secretary, yes I am an amazing secretary. If I ever fail in journalism then I'll be quite happy to go back to doing that because it was a job I loved and working for a huge office full of journalists who all had too much to do, not enough time, too many stories, who were throwing tasks at me. I'm still in touch with all of the people from those days and it was just a fantastic way of learning about things.

And also being good on the phone is a skill in journalism and in life, which is very overlooked. And nowadays it's all to do with emails and having people's mobiles and texting them, and I often say to young reporters in my team 'why don't you just phone them up because you might get more out of them if you have a conversation rather than just exchanging electronic messages?' And because I'd done telesales for years, I was very good at getting people on the phone, and when I became a reporter this was a definite advantage.

I can see that. Now Claer, I want to talk about a subject I know is close to your heart, and that is financial education. Your mission as you state it, is to de-mystify the world of finance, why do you think that is so important?

Well I think that large tranches of the financial services industry sadly have the mission of mystifying it for us so that we all then pay them to explain it back to us. And there are a lot of products, especially pensions, where the rules are very complicated but also the level of jargon involved just makes the average person switch off, not want to understand how things work, which means that they're going to get a worse deal.

But it's also the case in something like energy bills and choosing a tariff and there are hundreds and hundreds of different ones. Or even if you were to be quite advanced about your finances and pick a stocks and shares ISA for example, there are potentially many hundreds of funds or other products that you could choose to put into that product.

So having all of this choice is great, but it also means that we have to make a decision and my fear is that for a lot of people making no decision is the default option and that can actually be a much worse outcome than if they'd made a decision that perhaps wasn't the best, that was quite good, but making no decision at all, particularly when it comes to saving up money for the future.

Exactly, and one of the things I'm seeing people do since our great pension freedoms were introduced, is they're taking money out of a really tax efficient pension wrapper and sticking it in a high street bank account and getting 0.1% and thinking they've made a smart move.

But then if you look at the forces that are driving that perhaps, number one is stock markets around the world are falling, there's been some really heavy falls in the last few days at the time of speaking to you, which spooks people and they think well I'd rather get my money out and have it in cash. So its not just about understanding the stock market, it's about understanding the risk process and when you might need that money.

And the money in my stocks and shares ISA, well I'm 41 now and I know that things are going up and down, I haven't even looked at it in the last six weeks because I don't want to know. I've made my decisions and I will stand by them because I don't intend to take a penny out of that account until I am well over the age of 60 in an ideal world. It's nice to have it there in case something bad happens and I need it before then but you really have to think about investing in pensions in terms of decades instead of months.

But the people who are taking cash out and putting it in the High Street bank think that cash is safe. Women especially are real lovers of cash products, not just for themselves, also women are more likely to open junior ISAs in a family situation where there are children and they're also more likely to put those in cash, whereas that's an investment that's tied up for 18 years so it's just going to go backwards in terms of inflation.

It all comes back to decisions again, if you have to decide what funds to put your children's junior ISA in which fund do you choose, this one, that one, there are hundreds, I can't make a decision, the result, the default, do nothing and then their money goes backwards.

So how can we overcome this because I know particularly the financial education of women has been a topic that's close to your heart. And one of the tactics you've used for that, which seems to be working very well, is this concept of the online money diary. Tell me how that's worked.

Yes people talk about women's finances because there are lots of statistics about the gender pay gap and the gender pensions gap, which is related, and also the fact that fewer women actually invest than men. And I think we have to be very careful Graham about saying 'well women don't invest because they can't do it or they won't do it' - I don't think that's the case. There are many reasons that prevent women from investing; one of them could be that they're just not earning enough; a second one could be that they lack the confidence to do so and that they particularly want more face-to-face assurance from an advisor. That's come out in surveys as being much more important, whereas men might be happy to do their own research and do something online. And of course face-to-face financial advice is horrifically expensive in this country.

So in terms of why finance is such a crucial issue for women, the Editor of the Money Diaries website in America says that money is the last taboo holding back working women. And I think this is true because, as we've seen with the gender pay gap, how do you know what your colleagues are earning, whether they are female or male, do you have any idea about what process you need to go through in your company to get a pay rise, who you would need to ask, are you asking the right person, is there indeed a chance that you could move up, move sideways within the company, grow your career? These are all questions that women (and men) feel a bit shady about asking.

The whole idea of the Money Diaries is to give a woman an anonymous spending diary covering seven days at the outset of which they provide a rough balance sheet of their life, like how much they're earning, which is a question that you feel you can never ask people, and how much debt they have. I find people can often be more boastful about that in public company when it comes to talking about how big your mortgage is, but less so when it comes to credit card debt, which is seen as a source of shame. The diaries also ask them to clarify what they're spending on a day-to-day basis.

And it is absolutely addictive reading getting an insight into somebody's spending habits. It's particularly interesting if they are on a fantastic wage, say a tech worker in California or, on the other hand, if they don't have very much money and they are putting brunch on their credit card and the online commentators have a field day and say 'oh how could you do this?' But by reading about what our peers are doing and where they're going right and where they're going wrong, it has actually emerged there is a fantastic source of financial education without it being bound up, prescribed or put in some book. I get sent these dreadful books all the time about 'read this and become a money expert'. I just think the kind of people who need to read this book are never going to buy a book about becoming a money maestro let alone actually finish reading it!

These diaries are entertaining but they are also insightful, so you are reading about how other women are handling their money and getting ideas – these are by good or bad examples – and taking something away from that. So it's a completely new way of doing that and as the Financial Times Money Editor, I think that entertainment is a really important part of what we're doing in our journalism in the FT Weekend. If you're publishing articles that are quite dry and boring, yes the information has got to be correct, but in order for people, whether they're male or female, to want to read that article and apply it to their life, its got to be somewhat tantalising and interesting to read. It needs to answer the question what am I going to get out of this if I read this piece? Well you could feel a lot better about your finances rather than the big nagging finger of doom saying 'don't spend any money on avocados'.

Which brings me onto my next subject, which is moving on from women and the financial issue to the next generation. Again, talking about making it interesting, a lot of Millennials that I speak to or see interviewed seem to find the whole topic very dull and boring. So how can we get them more engaged in their financial education?

Well I'd go further than that Graham, I think they find it traumatic. Certainly the focus groups that we've done at the FT with younger readers, they're just pumped full of 'your generation is the one that's going to get it in the neck, your pensions are rubbish or non-existent, your salary, because you started a job in the recession, is never going to grow in any meaningful way, you're never going to be able to afford to buy a property, you're going to be renting this global asset class for the rest of your life'. So why would you try and be good with money, you may as well just spend it all on a nice holiday and Instagraming your avocado brunch or whatever?

I can totally understand that rejection and them saying 'well what's the point because we're never going to have the things that previous generations have had?' So there's a lot of negativity, but you have to try and build on that and say it's not as hopeless as you think and there are things that you can do. And one of the main ways that people can help themselves is by joining their workplace pension.

We do a presentation at the FT every year aimed at our younger staff, where we explain to people that paying into a pension actually costs a lot less than you might think because a) you pay less tax, you get tax relief and b) for the amount you put in your company will normally put in the same amount, match it or put in some more. So when you actually look at the numbers, which are very hard to get out of companies, what will the number in the bottom right hand corner of my paycheck actually show if I join the pension scheme?

Now that is the question I wish I'd known the answer to when I started my first job. I was trying to buy a house, I was saving up and I just thought 'hmm, I'm not going to do the company pension scheme' – big mistake.

I also thought that I would only be at that company for two years but in the end I was there for seven.

And of course I think what you said, even from your childhood, is if you can get into that discipline of saving regularly with the miracle of compounding and long-term investing, you can turn a small amount into a very big pension chunk for when you retire.

Absolutely and in my presentation that I do, I have a picture of a snowball off a mountain, because I think that's the best way of explaining compound interest. The earlier you start, even if you only have a snowball, by the time you retire, which let's face it, might not be until your late 70s or even 80s for some people the way we're going, that snowball would have grown. So even putting away small amounts, the industry is calling it 'micro investing' and there are now lots of apps where you can do things like round up your spare change so you're putting a couple of pounds a day into a stocks and shares ISA Moneybox. I just think it's, it's an innovative product and it's engaging with a new market of consumers who are very different from the ones that went before.

Well that's great advice to end our time together on, Claer Barrett, thank you very much indeed.

Thank you Graham

Three Key Lessons
From Claer Barrett

1. **Be Organised!** In your work and your finances. Claer used her organisational skills honed as a secretary to make her a more effective journalist and also to get on top of her personal finances. The most successful people on the planet have the same 24 hours a day as you do – the difference is how effectively you use the time to achieve your goals.

2. **Have a clear mission** – Claer knew early on that she wanted to de-mystify the world of finance for her readers so this helps her choose which topics to write about and how to explain them because she has a clear understanding of the kind of person she is writing for. Note how empathetic she is to the dilemma they face, for example in choosing a cash ISA rather than a stocks and shares product.

3. **Be careful with your money!** Claer's frugal parents ingrained this approach in her childhood which is when our thinking around money is formed. The only way you are certain of becoming wealthy is to form the habit of living within your means, saving and investing regularly. With compounding, even small amounts become millions if you start early enough.

Dominic Frisby

Dominic Frisby
Stand Up Comedian turned Gold and Crypto Expert

Dominic Frisby is a true one-off. How many people do you know whose CV boasts stand-up comedian, voice over actor, boxing compere, sitcom actor and financial writer?

The son of playwright Terence Frisby, he studied Italian and drama before finding work almost immediately as a voice over artist when he graduated. Radio and television followed, along with a chance meeting with the editor of Money Week which triggered his journalistic career.

Dominic is the author of two books – Life After The State is one of my all time favourites and should be read by everyone who values freedom and democracy. Bitcoin The Future of Money was one of the first books to take a serious look at cryptocurrencies on which Dominic believes the jury is still out.

He has two children by former wife Louisa Haye, sister of the boxer David Haye.

In 2019 Dominic was announced as the Brexit Party's Parliamentary candidate for Old Bexley and Sidcup.

In this chapter we meet someone who is a polymath; he's a voiceover artist, he's a financial journalist, he's a best selling author, he's an expert on cryptocurrencies and precious metals and perhaps best of all is known for writing in Money Week magazine. His name is Dominic Frisby. Dominic welcome to Money & Me.

Thank you very much Graham.

Now I know, in doing a little bit of research on your background, that your father was the playwright and novelist, Terence Frisby, whose work included the long-running theatre play, 'There's a Girl in My Soup'. Tell me a bit about what life was like growing up - the life of a writer can be a little bit financially precarious, so what was it like for you?

Well it can be and my dad still is Terence Frisby, he's still with us, and he wrote 'There's a Girl in My Soup' and I think he wrote it in maybe 1965 and it was put on in 1966 and I wasn't born until 1969, but it became the longest running comedy in the history of the West End; it broke all the records. Those records have since been overtaken but at the time it ran for six years and it made Michael Codron, who was the man who produced it, his fortune.

It was just unbelievably successful and you know my granddad worked on the trains, so my dad went from being a platelayer's son to becoming one of the richest people in the country; he became extraordinarily rich extraordinarily quickly.

And in the late 1960s they had, I think it was 98% income tax or whatever it was, and because he'd suddenly earned all this money he found he was going to have to give most of it back. So he actually became a tax exile, they went to Cannes in the South of France. I know all this because it's been told to me a million times but I wasn't actually there.

And then I was conceived in Cannes and that's why they gave me the name, Dominic, because they wanted to give me a sort of Frenchie name, but I think they wanted to call me Jean Paul or something like that but Jean Paul Frisby would have sounded a bit weird. So anyway I landed up with Dominic. And then the play was made into a film, which was very successful.

Then, unfortunately, my parents got involved in a very acrimonious divorce in the 1970s, and that extraordinary amount of money that my dad earned, by one way or another, some of it went to my mum but I don't think even half to her, most of it went to lawyers and to the taxman; he lost all his money again. So the big life lesson there is do not get divorced!

Right absolutely.

And often divorce is inevitable because you and your partner don't get on anymore and so the even bigger life lesson is to make sure you choose your partner very carefully!

Indeed, and it very rarely gets mentioned in an investment context, but that is absolutely true, divorce is one of the biggest destroyers of wealth ever. As Mr Bezos of Amazon fame might be about to find out as well..

Well yes. I have another close family member who was married for 32 years to her husband who was very old and about to die. She had contributed around two thirds of the couple's net worth and then they recently got divorced. Because of the divorce laws in the country the money was split 50/50 even though she's got a life expectancy of three or four times as long as he does. But his daughters agitated for this divorce because they wanted to take half her money through his inheritance if that makes sense. So the 50/50 law was designed to protect against that, but in fact it gets badly exploited, as most laws do.

So you grew up with that rather complex scenario, what were your own life or career plans as you reached adulthood?

I never had any really; I always had this vague idea that I would be a writer. I can remember my mum having dinner parties when I was about 15 and all these incredibly old people asking me what I wanted to do and I never really had any idea. I mean I've always had this vague idea that I'd like to be very successful and comfortably off but I've never quite known how.

Anyway, I went to university where I did Italian and drama because my mum was Italian and my dad was a dramatist, so it seemed like a logical thing to do. Then I was a bit clearer that I wanted to be a writer, but all the best writers, from Shakespeare to Dickens, all these great writers, they'd all started out as actors. So I had this idea that if I wanted to be a writer I needed to be an actor first. And so that's when I went to drama school.

Then, when I was at drama school, I found that I was the best at radio in the year group, I don't know why, but I was the best at radio. I made a tape and this voiceover artist got hold of the tape before I'd even left drama school and signed me to this voiceover agency. I had my first job within a week of leaving drama school and it was a one year contract presenting ATP tennis on Channel 4 with Andrew Castle, who has gone on to become a presenter on ITV and various other places. But just doing the voice for it and suddenly I was a voiceover artist and I've always done that since. But you know being a voiceover artist isn't full time work so there's always been plenty of time to write as well.

You also did a sitcom with Davina McCall, you played a gay salsa teacher in 'Murder in Suburbia', you had a million views of your 'Debt Bomb' video on YouTube, so I guess obviously from there a natural progression into financial journalism?

Well obviously! What happened was I carried on acting but what I hated about acting is that once the last job finishes the entire future is completely dark, you've just got no idea. And the insecurity of it drove me insane. Whereas voiceovers, which is even more insecure because I don't even know what tomorrow's jobs are until tea time today, but for some reason, because there was a constant flow of work I was always more comfortable with it. And you're treated very well doing voiceovers, you're treated like royalty and even if you don't get treated like a big start you earn good money.

Anyway, by the mid-noughties, I'd earned a bit of money and I wanted to invest it and I started reading various things online and I became convinced that gold was the place to be, and it was in that decade. But then gold is a very political metal because it used to be money and it raised all these political issues, which I found incredibly interesting. And there were all these people that I wanted to meet and talk to and I thought how do I get to meet them, if I want to just hire them for an hour for their advice its going to cost me £200, £300, £500 every time and I'm not going to do that. At the same time the fund managers I spoke to about investing my money, they always wanted their little clips and I just thought I don't trust that.

So I started a podcast as a means to interview these guys and meet them. And, of course, everyone's busy pushing their own brand, so they were all quite happy to come and talk on the podcast. I discovered that podcasting is the best way to meet people - in the intensified environment of an interview you build up a relationship much more quickly because you have to get to the point more quickly.

So I just met loads of people. One of the people I met was Merryn Somerset Webb, who was (and is) the Editor of Money Week and she said 'oh we need people like you to come and write a column for us', and I said 'well I don't really think so, you know I'm a comedian' – I'd begun a career as a comedian on the side – I don't really think I should do this. And Merryn said 'no, no, no we need people who can talk about finance in a language that people understand'.

So the podcast proved very popular because I was asking the questions that everyday people have on their minds and the column proved very popular and that's how I ended up writing about finance.

I see. So you write about gold but also you started investing in it and I think clearly at that time you were not just investing in the metal, I think you were also looking at the miners who produced the metal?

Yes.

So that was an interesting and a somewhat higher risk scenario perhaps?

Well I don't think I quite understood the risks that I was taking, but I invested a lot in physical gold and silver and in fact I had various properties which I sold to invest in gold and silver. And for a while that proved a brilliant investment. And then, what I didn't see coming out of the financial crisis was the slashing of interest rates and everything else like quantitative easing and the big boom in property that came between about 2010 and 2015. I missed out on that and I've never quite forgiven myself.

What I didn't understand about mining is I was led to believe that if you invested in a mining company it gave you optionality on gold and silver, it was like buying an option on gold and silver. What I didn't understand was the actual risk of mining itself, how much can go wrong, whether it's running a functioning mine or exploring for the metal itself. And you read that this guy's drilled here and he's found this much rock in the ground and you think yeah great, but you don't realise the multitude of problems that the guy is going to have getting it out of the ground.

I was investing in mining companies and doing quite well out of it for quite a long time, but without actually realising what can go wrong. That I would discover later...

Okay, so you were in mining and gold itself at that point. Where did you take it from there in terms of broadening out and diversifying your investment portfolio?

Well I haven't diversified anything like as much as I should do. And I feel that diversification is a means of protecting wealth, whereas if you actually want to make money you need to concentrate on one particular area. But the problem with that is if you concentrate on the wrong area you also lose a lot of money.

Right!

But if you diversify, say you do the Marc Faber thing where you're 25% in precious metals, 25% in bonds, 25% in real estate and 25% in equities - there's your diversified portfolio in very simple terms. The bond market could be doing very well for a bit and the real estate market could be suffering, well in terms of your overall portfolio you're fine because you're diversifying. But in terms of wealth building, if you want to make a fortune you've got to find a bull market, get in early and then get out near the top.

Right yes.

It sounds easy.

I think you're telling me that you didn't quite manage to succeed in the gold sector with that timing?!

At one point you made so much money in mining because you could literally buy stocks and they'd go up five times. And I had one stock that went from $1 to $30, can you imagine.

Wow!

But now it's trading at $4.

Hmm, a bit volatile.

So you did all the way up and all the way down. And I had only ever experienced a bull market, I'd never experienced a bear market and so I didn't see the signs early enough and I didn't get out early enough. And now, when people talk to me about mining and gold and bull markets and things like that, I feel, having lived through the mining bear market, I'm the most wise as to the nature of bear markets - they are vicious, horrible things.

I got into cryptocurrencies very early and I did very well out of that, but now Bitcoin is in a massive bear market (*this was before the Bitcoin bounce in the first half of 2019 – GR*) and all these guys are losing fortunes and I'm kind of sitting there going, it's a bear market, it can be a lot more horrible than you think! And you know I'm not liked for saying it but I've seen it in mining, I know what can happen.

Dominic - you've been through the ups and downs twice now with gold and then cryptos, where do you see the cryptocurrency market going from here?

The answer to that question Graham is there are two ways it can go and it depends on your view of how unique and special the technology behind Bitcoin is. Now if Bitcoin really is going to be the default money system of the internet it will have extraordinary value. If blockchain technology is really going to transform everything from financial markets to the way we vote to the legal system, as many of its advocates say it will, then it will have extraordinary value. But if it's just another kind of flash in the pan technology then we're going to be in this bear market for quite a long time.

But even something like the internet, which really did change the world, the mass tech, which is sort of the index of the internet if you like, only regained its dot com highs three or four years ago, so it can take that long - 15 years or so. That said, if you bought Amazon, Apple, Google, Microsoft, any of these kinds of companies in 2002/2003 you made your money back many times over.

If you look at 3D stocks, there was a huge bubble in 3D stocks in around about 2014. And there's one company, 3D Systems, you could have bought it for $1 in 2009 and sold it for $95 in 2014. And 3D technology is going to change the world, 3D printing, we're all going to just download the software onto our printer and print out whatever we want. You can build a house with a 3D printer in China for $10,000. Incredible possibilities, everyone is really excited.

And then you realise Amazon are already delivering products within six hours, do I even need a 3D printer? Where am I going to put a 3D printer and what about the problems I have with my ordinary Hewlett Packard printer – it's always jamming and it doesn't connect to the internet properly. Think of the problems you have with your current printer and that's just using paper - what kind of problems are you going to have with a 3D printer?

So suddenly everyone was saying maybe 3D printing isn't all that special. And so that $95 stock went all the way back to $6 in 2015 and here we are in 2019 and it's at $9. The bear market went on for four or five years.

The question with Bitcoin is if it really is special we'll have a big washout. Was 2017 Bitcoin's dot com moment or is Bitcoin's dot com moment still to come and 2017 was the internet in 1995? That's the big question that's still out there.

So would you be putting new money into cryptocurrencies today?

Well I am putting new money into it. I've just become a Director of a Canadian company, which has been set up specifically to invest in privacy technologies, including privacy coins, and I've put a lot of my own money into it and I think that privacy is going to be the narrative which drives the next big bull market in technology.

If you think how important privacy is and how we've given it away without realising it. Think of all the manipulation that goes on with Facebook data in elections and so on, there's maybe even going to be government regulations demanding certain privacy requirements and that cost is going to end up being passed on to the consumer. One way or another privacy is going to change, the value of privacy.

Absolutely and you mentioned the government there and in your book, 'Life After the State' you talk about how you think society should be run and obviously we're going through all kinds of stuff at the moment with Brexit etc. What do you think are the fundamentals that need to change in the way we run our country and what are the kind of lessons that you'd want to see learnt coming out of Life After the State?

Well I've just finished the first draft of my next book, which is called 'Daylight Robbery: The Past Present and Future of Taxation', and in that I've written a big chapter on the incredible success story that is Hong Kong. You have no idea how penniless that country was in 1945 and now its GDP per capita is three times of the average person in the UK. It is extraordinarily rich and it was so successful so quickly that Singapore copied it, South Korea copied it, Japan copied it, and even China copied it.

People thought when Hong Kong was put back in China in 1998 that that would be the end of Hong Kong – no, it was the end of China! That's how powerful the Hong Kong model is and it was built on low taxes and simple taxes. Even today tax lawyers agree that Hong Kong has the best tax code in the world. It is 1.5% the length of the British tax code, 1.5%!

And tax revenue, they never spent before they earnt, there was never any debt, tax revenue was always around about 15% of GDP, about 40% of tax revenue came from land taxes rather than income taxes, income taxes only affected the highest earners, never more than 15%. Low rates of corporation tax attract investment and almost all of it was down to this one man called Cowperthwaite, a Scottish adherent of Adam Smith who was Hong Kong's Financial Secretary.

John James Cowperthwaite; he was Deputy Financial Secretary and if you listen to his speeches in the Hong Kong Assembly they're so funny and they're so kind of Thatcheresque but he refused to compile GDP data because 'it will only be used against me'. And eventually he came under all this pressure to compile GDP data and so he hired this academic to compile the data and for seven years this poor man kept giving him revisions of the data and Cowperthwaite would say no it's flawed because of this reason, flawed because of that reason. And after seven years the academic eventually resigned and Cowperthwaite went back to the Hong Kong Assembly and said it's not working, the GDP data is not working and it's because the whole idea is flawed.

He'd set this poor man up to be a fall guy, but you know he achieved all these things in a quite authoritarian way - Hong Kong wasn't a democracy, it was a British colony and obviously China is also authoritarian.

And Singapore.

Yes, and they're all authoritarian countries but in terms of what their economies have achieved and in the space of time they've achieved it, it's amazing.

So if I'm Prime Minister, the first thing I will do is simplify the tax system and model a new tax system on Hong Kong. And you know I really think taxation is the 'Patient Zero', - you determine the destiny of a country by the way you tax it. Our tax system is overly complicated, it gets manipulated, it gets abused, people cheat it, there's loads of subsidies that favour some people against other people, there's so much that is iniquitous.

So my big thing would be to reform tax and then let everything else take care of itself.

That brings me onto the other big question hanging in the air at the moment, I'm guessing with that sort of a manifesto you're probably not going to get offered a job by Jeremy Corbyn if he comes into power, so what might happen to us if we have a Corbyn/McDonnell government?

We will tax ourselves into oblivion I fear. McDonnell is actually in favour of land taxes and I support him on that, but he's in favour of land taxes in addition to other taxes. I would have land taxes to replace other taxes. But I don't think you need worry about a Corbyn government Graham, I don't think the British people will vote for it.

I think there's far too much apathy about this, I think what they'll do is they'll vote for change, a bit like America did with Trump, it doesn't necessarily matter who the person is or what they say their policies are, they're just going to want something different from the status quo.

Jeremy Corbyn does not have the charisma of Donald Trump. What does Jeremy Corbyn think about Brexit, he never says and, you know, people need leadership. Donald Trump would not only be holding court about Brexit, even if he totally contradicted himself one week to the next, he'd be holding court about it, he'd be saying this, he'd be slagging off the EU, he'd be making ridiculous demands on the EU, then he'd be going look, they can't meet my demands and he would do a deal, some kind of deal. And you can say what you like about Trump but he does deals.

Yes absolutely.

He sorted out the EU and within an hour he came to an agreement with Juncker. So I don't think the comparison between Jeremy Corbyn and Donald Trump is valid. I will accept your point that Britain might want change, but we're in an era of strong man leaders. Countries want strong man leaders and Britain craves some kind of strong man leader, but I don't think Jeremy Corbyn is a strong man leader. (*Between recording this interview when Theresa May was in Downing Street and publishing the transcripts as a book Britain now has a blond, strong man leader in Boris Johnson – GR*)

You're probably right, but thinking about the longer term perspective, you've got your own children growing up now, what are you going to teach them about money and investing that perhaps was lacking in your own financial education?

The power of compounding is like no other power on earth. It is, as Einstein said, the eight wonder of the world. And you know I've already got my kids junior ISAs and I'm trying to get them to monitor it and keep adding to it. Rather than give them pocket money straight into their current account, I put half the pocket money into their savings account and half into their current account and then when there's a big pile in the savings account I move it into the junior ISA, so that there's a constant kind of compounding effect.

But unfortunately the wisdom of the power of compounding is not understood by the young - if only it was!

Well perhaps you can tell them a bit more about it as they grow up so they'll have a little nest egg already put away. Dominic Frisby thank you very much for joining us.

Thank you Graham.

Three Key Lessons
From Dominic Frisby

1. **Divorce is the greatest destroyer of wealth** – so choose your life partner carefully and do everything you can to stay together! The dilemma was highlighted by the late Country singer Tammy Wynette whose two greatest hits were 'Stand by your man' and 'D.I.V.O.R.C.E.'

2. **Focus to build wealth, diversify to protect wealth** – not everyone will agree with this one because it's a high risk approach. Choose the right company or sector and you could make a fortune, choose badly and you could set your plan back years. My own approach uses a Wealth Pyramid with different assets at different levels of the pyramid doing a different job for me.

3. **Compounding is the 8th wonder of the world** – nothing new here, but it bears repeating because so few people seem to recognise it and exploit it. Even saving modest sums with average returns can turn into a substantial nest egg if you start young enough. Compounding works on a hockey stick shape so the biggest gains come at the very end. Take a multi-generational view of wealth creation and your family can benefit massively from a plan that covers 30, 40 or 50 years of wealth building.

John Stepek

John Stepek
Teaching Us To Be Sceptical Investors.

John Stepek is the executive editor of Money Week, Britain's best selling weekly investment magazine. He is also the main writer on the daily email series Money Morning.

After working in the family business in Glasgow, John moved into a journalistic career after studying psychology at university and has found this invaluable in understanding how badly suited the human brain is to the demands of investing. This is reflected in his book The Sceptical Investor which encourages us to engage our brain rather than our gut when making investment decisions.

Money Week correctly predicted the 2008 financial crisis before many other commentators and often takes a contrarian position.

John has written for The Spectator and The Sunday Times and has appeared as an expert commentator on BBC Radio 4's Today programme, BBC Radio Scotland, Newsnight, Daily Politics and Bloomberg.

My guest in this chapter is one of the UK's leading financial journalists and for some years now he's been Executive Editor of the best selling financial magazine in the country, Money Week. He's also just published his first book, 'The Sceptical Investor'. His name is John Stepek; John welcome to Money & Me.

Thanks for having me Graham.

Now what you may not realise is this 48th floor studio is actually a time machine and we can use it to just whisk you back to your childhood and ask you a little bit about the family circumstances you grew up in and whether things like money were even discussed?

I was lucky enough to have a fairly comfortable background. My mother was a teacher, she stopped doing that when we were born and so became a housewife. My dad ran a small business, which his father had founded, so it was a family business basically selling televisions and couches in parts of Glasgow and the surrounding areas.

So we were brought up to be aware that we were lucky basically. We went on nice holidays. Money was never something that we had to worry about and there was always that sense that that was a privilege and that it took a lot of hard work. There was also a sense that we shouldn't take it for granted, though not in a heavy-handed way. I guess the thing is my parents both grew up in less well-off families, because my dad, he was the eldest of ten kids and at that time my granddad was just setting up the business. So they all lived in a wee flat in Cambuslang, which is a town near Glasgow and my mum was brought up in a council house. Again, her parents both worked, it's not as if I'm saying they were really badly off or anything, but our circumstances were much better than theirs when they were growing up. I think that there's always that sense of how do you stop your kids from being spoilt, how do you stop them from taking things for granted and I think that's always the case whenever you feel that your kids are getting maybe a more privileged upbringing than you did.

Right okay so at what point did the potential interest of your own in things like money, investing and journalism develop?

I always wanted to be a writer, if I'm absolutely honest, even when I was a wee kid. In fact one of my earliest memories is scribbling, I couldn't write but I was trying to write a story about Scooby-Doo and I must have been about 3 or 4. And so that's always been something that I was interested in.

As far as the money side of things went, as I was growing up the family business was very much a presence in the background because we lived on the premises, so the office was directly across from where we lived and most of my dad's siblings worked in the business as well. So, although my mum and dad always told us we should do what we wanted to do, all the time I was growing up I was thinking I wonder if I should go into the business? There was always that sense of, on the one hand that would have been an easy way to get a job, on the other hand there was a certain sense of that's what you should do - even though, as I say, my parents weren't at all suggesting we go in that direction.

So there was interest in business from that point of view, but then I went to university where I studied psychology and business studies, a slightly odd combination. I found psychology much more interesting and, after a couple of years, I worked in the TV industry trying to make it as a scriptwriter, but that didn't happen for various reasons. Then I got married and I realised that I needed to do something that's a proper job and I went and retrained as a journalist. I realised, if I want to make a living from writing, that's one way to do it, it's not a very respectable way to do it but it's a way to do it. And then I specialised in finance because that was a topic I was already curious about and it also meant I wouldn't have to do anything unpleasant like doorstop people. I didn't want to be a pure news journalist.

It's interesting you studied psychology because I think you've gone on to write about how so many aspects of the human psyche make us very ill-prepared to be effective investors.

Oh yes definitely, I mean I did find psychology fascinating and when I was a young guy, I don't know why I was in such a hurry but basically I didn't enjoy formal education that much. I didn't play up in class or anything, I just didn't really like the strictness of school. And I felt that I had to go to university to get a degree to get a good job, but before I'd gone I hadn't really known what I wanted to do and honestly I was just keen to get it over with. Again, I don't know why, I just wanted to get into the world. So it took me a long time to appreciate that I actually did enjoy psychology and I had thought about taking it on but I knew I'd have to do more studying for that and I just didn't want to do that.

I've certainly come back to psychology a lot in investment. One of the reasons I wrote the book about contrarian investing is that it's all about trying to stop yourself from making stupid mistakes. And so much of investment, there's things that you know and then there are mistakes that you just keep making even though you know this stuff. And I think it's really important to try and help people, if you like, untangle the knots in their head because we're not designed to be good investors, our minds are not set up for it.

You can talk about evolutionary biology or put it in any context you want, but really the issue is that investing is complicated, it involves a fair bit of luck and it's also not consistent enough in terms of the patterns that repeat. Unlike something like chess, it's very hard to get a good intuition for it. So often when your gut is telling you to do something, it's actually totally the wrong thing when it comes to investing. You've got to deploy your brain first but when we're dealing with money we get panicky.

Well that's true because one of our guests on the programme (Siam Kidd – GR) is an expert in trading the financial markets and he talked to me about what he calls the 90-90-90 rule, which is 90% of traders lose 90% of their capital in 90 days, which is not a great starting point!

Yes I'm intrigued; the behavioural stuff is at its strongest in trading – I know because experimented with spread betting. One of the reasons is because I don't ever like writing about something that I haven't at least tried myself - because a lot of the time you find that whenever you do something then the practice is very different to what you might have written in the paper. And so I would highly suggest that people don't spread bet just to be clear okay!

I tried it and what I found was fascinating was the emotional rush that you get from it. It's so immediate, it's very compelling and it's quite addictive. But there's also the fact that it doesn't matter that you've promised yourself that you won't do this or you won't do that, something happens in the market and suddenly you're down £500 or £600. You're thinking 'what just happened there?' and immediately looking at chasing the loss rather than shutting it down and suddenly you're doing all the things that you know you shouldn't do. You just aren't in control of yourself at that specific moment.

So I think being able to bypass or short circuit your worst instincts is a really important thing for an investor, and I actually talk about that quite a lot in the book.

Are you closer to the Bill Bonner mindset which is make one investment decision per decade?

I think that's sensible, if you can get away with that I think that's a good idea. And I also think for most people investing really shouldn't be that hard. Most people are not keen to actively manage their own investments. That's not to say that you can't do a DIY portfolio, but these days it's very easy to get broad exposure to stocks, bonds, property, a couple other asset classes and then just invest every month, take it out when you retire and that's all you need to do. Make sure that it's low cost and you should build a decent enough pot over time.

If you do want to be a more active investor, which I think is great as well, and obviously that's who Money Week is often writing to, it's just worth being aware of all the obstacles that are in your way and having a good idea how to overcome them.

Well I think one of the underlying issues, which you certainly try and address through your writing, is the lack of financial education in this country - we don't learn this stuff at school or university do we?

We don't, I mean I have mixed feelings about financial education in the classroom and the reason for that is that I think that for most people, when they really need the information is almost at the point of sale. I remember getting taught about utility bills for example at school and you know that it may be useful for the future but at the end of the day the electricity company works out your bills so why do I need to work out how many units I've used? And I can't help but feel that it would be yet another subject that for most kids, okay I've done an exam in that and then they forget about it until they need it and at that point it's all changed anyway, like with the mortgage industry for example.

I'm not saying we shouldn't have financial education but I think we have to think about when we provide it much more clearly. And also I think we need to make it much more basic. Perhaps talk about principles rather than for example pensions; 'pensions' is an off-putting word. If you're going to make a list of the ten most boring words in the English language pensions would be number one.

True.

Honestly you don't put the word 'pension' in a headline because nobody will click on it, it's a boring word, it's depressing. So I think what we need to get across is that over your lifetime you have to save money so that when you're not working you've got money to live off. That's it, that's what we need to know.

The trouble is though, then you get someone like George Osborne comes along with his so-called pension freedoms and now we learn two or three years later that over a million people have been caught out. So it feels to me like there is a time of life where a bit of education might help.

I agree with that but it's a time of life issue, because the other problem is that you're right, George Osborne came along and changed that and some of those changes were good, but the problem is that before him, Gordon Brown came along and changed it and before him Tony Blair and Gordon Brown changed it again. So we now have an entirely different pension system to the one we had 20 years ago and we also had a different pension system then to the one we had 20 years before that.

Though many people didn't have to worry about their pension. For example I work around my home town in Kent and I remember we'd just moved there ten years ago and I kept bumping into men in their 50s or early 60s, clearly retired, just doing odd jobs or pottering about in the garden and I was starting to wonder where these guys have made enough money to retire? The vast majority of them were ex-BT workers so they had nice occupational pensions and you'd look at them and you're thinking good on you, but on the other hand, I will never ever save enough in my pension pot to have as good a pension as you've got right now!

Even if you saved the maximum permitted by law you wouldn't get more than £25k a year on an annuity.

Yes right. I think the other problem is that this pensions thing is ever-changing - I can see why people get put off because every single budget someone else has got their hands in there and they're messing about. Imagine if, for example, and this is not to be party political about it, but if we go from the current Government to a Labour Government who are more radically left wing you can imagine that the pension system may change drastically again.

So it's not just about education, it's about the fact that the politicians keep pulling the rug out from under us and I think we could do with less of that though I don't know how you'd do it!

Let's talk about that small topic, the 2008 financial crisis. John, there's that famous quote from the Queen visiting the London School of Economics and asking why did nobody see this coming? I think you would take issue with that narrative.

Yes I certainly feel our own magazine did mention that a few times in the run up to the financial crisis that there were going to be problems with credit. And, to be fair, we were by no means the only ones. One reason that I was paying attention to it was because Gillian Tett at the FT was writing a lot of columns about the problems in the US subprime market. And people had been looking for ways to short US housing for a long time. Again the guys in the Big Short are the ones that get the kudos but they weren't the only ones.

So it was clear that we were coming up to some sort of crunch and I remember in mid-2007 we had a cover in the magazine saying 'here comes the credit crunch' and there was a cartoon on the front page of an investor in the jaws of a crocodile. And that was before Northern Rock went bust and also before the Icelandic Banks went bust.

I don't think it was as difficult to see coming as the prevailing narrative has it. The LSE economists didn't tell the Queen that, obviously! I wish we'd sent Her Majesty a copy of that issue of Money Week…

Yes you should have done shouldn't you. But I suppose really the $64,000 question is have we learned the lessons from that crisis and are we in danger of something similar or even worse happening again today?

I think this is an interesting question. I feel that history doesn't tend to repeat itself when it comes to booms and busts in that each crisis is different from the one that came before it. That doesn't mean I don't think we're going to face another crisis at some point, but I think that people are currently primed for 2008 to happen again. I tend to think the next crisis will be an inflationary one and I'll explain why I think that.

After 2008 Central Banks printed a load of money and drove up asset prices, which essentially affects the banks' balance sheets, not so much in the Eurozone but certainly in the UK and the US. That has left us slightly mired in this situation where so much capital has been mis-allocated that we have companies that shouldn't still exist and couldn't survive at higher interest rates. We also have low productivity, which is I reckon, although it's debated, a direct result of low interest rates, which favour hiring employees over investing in machinery that would improve efficiency. So we're left in a situation of thinking how are we going to get out of this?

Another result of 2008 and the actions that were taken then is the political turmoil we're seeing just now. And the main knock-on effect of that, if we don't get it under control and get people happy with the way things are going again, is that there'll be more and more pressure on Governments to directly print money and give it to people. And this is why we're seeing it in America with the rise of Alexandria Ocasio-Cortez and talk of a theory called MMT (*Modern Monetary Theory – GR*), which I won't go into except to say it is just printing money and giving it to people rather than giving it to banks.

Now you might say what's wrong with that, I mean the banks got bailed out, why shouldn't the people...

This is Ben Bernanke's helicopter money isn't it?

Yes helicopter money, that's it. It's certainly been talked about a lot more. When it happens, if it doesn't work at first, they will just keep doing it until it does work. At that point you do get inflation, probably quite high inflation, but I'm not sure we're even going to need to get to that point. Because at the moment wage inflation is taking a long time to take off, but it's gradually taking off both here and in the US and even in Japan. Now we've got pretty much full employment in most of the world's biggest economies, at some point that has to turn into inflation and I think the issue then is that most people in the market are still terrified of deflation.

I think in a way one of the biggest drivers of inflation would be some sort of normalisation of interest rates, but the FED seems to have thrown in the towel already.

Well that's because the FED is terrified of the idea of normalising rates, but I actually think that normalising rates would be the healthiest thing they could do just now and I do think, if they want to get healthy inflation going, that's probably what they need to do.

I've been thinking about ways to think of this as a metaphor and I think it's almost like sharpening a knife on a whetstone; essentially we've got a blunt whetstone and we keep on going like that and think how come this knife's not getting any sharper? And it's because the problem is with the Central Bank policy of going in the wrong direction, they're suppressing activity by keeping rates this low.

But they seem to be more driven by whether their action has a negative impact on the Stock Market or if the President sends a particular kind of tweet we're going to change our strategy again overnight. So how do we get out of this?

It is difficult especially whenever they are as focused as they are on the level of the S&P. To be fair to Powell, I don't think that he's necessarily that bothered by what Trump tweets or doesn't tweet, it's just it's always going to be easier for Central Bankers to cut rates than raise them because cutting rates is popular and raising rates is not. Most of their colleagues in the economics profession can't see why we would raise interest rates when there's no inflation because they've got this very academic view of how things work. They don't want to get slighted at dinner parties by their colleagues or, the worst thing of all, is if they send the economy back into recession. Then everyone would say to them 'oh wait, you said you wouldn't do that back in the 1930s and you've made the exact same mistake again'.

So yes, I think the bias is always going to be towards much lower rates.

Okay so let's turn to your new book. There's a little bit of a clue in the title, 'The Sceptical Investor', but tell me what is the underlying message of the book?

Basically it's about contrarian investing, which I've slightly cheekily rebranded 'sceptical investing'. I've done that for a couple of reasons, it's not just to try and make a catchy title for the book. 'Contrarian investing' - everybody talks about it and there are lots of associations and clichés attached to it that I think aren't really that helpful. So the basic idea is that contrarian investing is going against the market, but the problem with that is that the market is often right, so always going against the market is going to be a losing strategy. You have to adopt some guidelines as to when you go against the market and when you don't.

The other reason is because, for example, value investing as a strategy is quite concrete, you know what it is, you buy cheap stocks and wait till they go up. And momentum investing is a strategy; you buy stuff that's going up and hope that it keeps going up, which often works. But contrarian investing isn't specifically that, it's more of a mindset and that's why I have rebranded it as sceptical investing.

So is there any difference between sceptical and contrarian?

Well I suppose it's just the way that I've framed it. What I'm talking about is how you should think about the market. The only thing that doesn't change in the market is the fact that it's humans that are in it and our behavioural flaws are the things that drive the cycles that we see.

I think if people take one thing away from the book in terms of the psychology of human beings, it's that we have this tendency to 'pattern spot', and that's just engrained in us, it's how we stay alive and how we navigate the world. We have to work out - well if that happens and that happens then that's going to happen, therefore I should or should not do it.

The problem is that that doesn't work well in investment because it leads to a tendency to extrapolate, so you see in straight lines, whereas markets and economies move in cycles. You tend to find that people are most euphoric when they should actually be most concerned. When the sky is blue everyone wants to invest, whenever it's chucking it down nobody wants to invest; you should be the opposite to that. And that's why I think the most important thing to remember is how human psychology affects the market.

The other thing that I really find fascinating is how quickly narratives change in markets but then become the accepted wisdom. So the story changes and then all of a sudden everyone thinks, 'oh that's the way it always was'.

True, one of the things I'm seeing at the moment is masses and masses of money being piled into tracker funds and similar products. You've already said that's definitely an investment strategy but it makes me think is this now the perfect time to go against the crowd and become a contrarian?

Yes I mean I think there are opportunities that arise from the influx into passive. I think that the way that it's presented is a bit misleading. We have this dichotomy between passive and active management, so the idea is if you don't want to go passive you should go active, but that's not the case. I think tracker funds are great, I think if you get a choice between investing in an S&P 500 tracker for example or a large cap American Stock Market fund run by an active Manager, you should definitely go for the passive option. It's cheap and this active guy is not going to beat the market consistently so you might as well get the market return if you believe that the US Stock Market is worth investing in.

Really these funds are just tools to express your view on markets. If you like Japan, will I buy an investment trust or an OEIC (*Open Ended Investment Company – GR*) or a tracker fund? Well look at them and see which one suits you best. That is fine.

Where I would say the issue is is this, because of the mania for tracker funds and indexing just now, what we're finding is a huge number of indices being created so that they can have funds that track them. And what I can see definitely happening, particularly amongst the slightly more fancy tracker funds, maybe low volatility funds or ones that are based on various factoral strategies, I can see that people may buy them thinking they're going to deliver one thing, but in fact they haven't looked into the small print or they haven't figured out exactly what they're really betting on, and I think that's probably where you've got the potential for this all to go wrong and for capital to be misallocated.

Okay. So I think in summary then what we're saying is these passive funds have their place, but also don't forget there's some huge opportunities if you're willing to go against the crowd and become a bit of a contrarian or at least a sceptical investor?

Yes absolutely, a good example is this: at the moment the UK is among one of the cheapest markets in the world, it's in the top 12 cheapest in the world or something like that next to Portugal. So, if you're looking for a good investment, then the UK is a contrarian investment now. It doesn't matter if you buy a tracker or an active fund, that's still a contrarian way to invest your money.

Brilliant, well that's some great advice to end on, John Stepek, thank you very much.

Thanks.

Three Key Lessons
From John Stepek

1. **Invest with your brain, not your gut.** We are not genetically programmed to make good investment decisions. We need to engage our brain and have a clear strategy that we can stick to without panicking if prices move against us.

2. **Financial education needs to be timely.** There's no point in learning about mortgages or utility bills at school because everything will have changed by the time you actually need to choose between suppliers. Even learning about pensions in adulthood is challenging because the politicians keep moving the goal posts.

3. **Be prepared to go against the crowd.** You can't just blindly do the opposite all the time, but there will be occasions when the crowd is wrong and you can make a lot of money with an opposite strategy. Perhaps the biggest example of this is the small group who bet against the US housing market in 2006/2007 as captured in the film and book The Big Short.

Section 4

The Coaches

Nicole Bremner

Dan Bradbury

Siam Kidd

John Howard

Nicole Bremner

Nicole Bremner

From Stay at Home Mum to Property Empire

Brought up as one of four children by a single mum in Australia, Nicole Bremner became the youngest person ever to qualify as a financial adviser in her home country. Love brought her to Britain and even to Goldman Sachs on Wall Street, before settling in Hackney and looking for a business she could run while bringing up her three kids.

The answer was to renovate her main home then an investment apartment. She caught the bug and developed partnerships that have helped her take on bigger projects and parlay her initial cash pile into a portfolio worth over £100 million.

She pioneered the use of crowdfunding property development projects and broke the world record by raising £1.62 million in 17 minutes!

She has captured the lessons she learned in her book, Bricking It, and is a regular speaker at property events as well as hosting a popular podcast.

My guest in this chapter has gone from being a stay-at-home mum with three kids eight years ago, to now sitting on top of a property empire worth £100 million. Her name is Nicole Bremner. Nicole welcome to Money & Me.

Thank you for having me.

I think your story actually starts in Australia, where you qualified originally as a financial planner, so tell me about how that worked out and your career in the regulated investment world.

I started out in medicine actually, I started off at university doing first year medicine with the idea of becoming a dentist; I thought that would be a great career. And in my first break in summer I got a job in a stockbroking firm and realised that I could earn a lot of money and not do seven years of study! So I switched majors into finance and got a full time job in that stockbroking firm, started my qualifications to become a financial planner and studied full time as well.

I didn't realise it at the time but I became the youngest qualified Chartered Financial Planner in Australia.

Wow, cool. And did you actually enjoy the work once you got into it?

I loved it, I found it really fascinating. I was never client facing, I was just too young, I was 19/20 at the time, but I loved looking at the portfolios and looking at investment strategies and weighing up how people should allocate their funds.

But I think romance got in the way and brought you across to Great Britain not long after that?

Yes exactly, I met a man and the lure of Europe was too great. I always wanted to live abroad and when he asked me if I'd come abroad with him I jumped at it and moved.

Okay, so I imagine that meant your qualifications were no longer relevant in London so what did you do as your next career move at that point?

It was really difficult because I came over here, I hadn't quite finished my degree, I'd finished the financial qualification but it was worthless over here, it was the year 2000 so the dot-com bubble had well and truly burst and it was really, really challenging.

I did get a job in a bank writing research reports, which I enjoyed but it wasn't really what I was passionate about. But gradually over time I proved myself and was able to work my way up in banking, though I was never really that great at banking.

But I think in the end you started to try and have your own business and you started various ventures with mixed results?

Yes again I tried a lot of things and I was really fortunate that I was in a position where I could try things. And my last job was Goldman Sachs on Wall Street, we lived in New York for a couple of years and that was just fascinating. Again, I started at Goldman on the day that Lehman Brothers collapsed in 2008 and it was just fascinating and frightening to sit and watch Fox News and CNN as the markets collapsed in front of me. I realised that with one very young child plus another one on the way, I couldn't go back into banking and I needed to look at other options.

I just didn't know what to do. I tried teaching knitting and crocheting, I tried being a food writer and photographer, I tried fashion and they were all marginally successful but nothing really paid any money. You put so much effort into these things and to not earn anything was quite demoralising.

Hmm and I think that's one of the things that people don't realise, especially when they have this culture shock of coming from a big corporation to running a small business when you are everything. You wear all the hats and you're the strategist but you're also the one that has to take out the rubbish. So you went through that, but I imagine it was a really useful learning process.

It definitely was because as you say, you end up being the HR department and the IT department and when things don't go right you're the only one that's there to fix it. And it can also be quite lonely. Luckily I like the solitude, I like working alone, but having worked in these big banking environments to then work on your own is very interesting. There are certain parts from the banking and corporate world that I was able to put into those things such as forecasting my finances and working out very quickly when a company is or is not working and the systems that need to be in place in order to make a business viable.

Right, and the reality is obviously most of these small start ups don't succeed, so it is a challenge. So you've tried several businesses now, none of them has quite worked out the way you were expecting, so what next; where do you go from this point?

Well I moved back to London in 2009. I then had a second child very quickly after the first, within 16 months, and I found this derelict vicarage in Hackney. I never thought I'd live in Hackney, I was living in Clerkenwell at the time, but the draw of this house was just too great and I decided to really get stuck into this huge renovation project. And it was a 4,000 sq ft house.

So I renovated this property and had another child, my third child during that process. And I absolutely loved it, I really enjoyed working with the builders, I enjoyed the creativity, I did all of it myself. My builder was as green as I was, so we were both learning on the job and it was just a fascinating experience that I really, really enjoyed.

I was still thinking 'what am I going to do when I grow up?' and it was at that point that my partner said to me, why don't you look at property? I'm sure you could do this as a living, you know everything about Hackney and every property that's going up for sale and has sold, why don't you invest in one? And that's really how the property business started.

Okay, so you've renovated what is your main home now and then your next project becomes your first investment - what kind of property was that?

The first thing I did was have a look at a flat that we'd owned in Clerkenwell that we'd had before the children, and I soon realised that that flat had earned more than I had working at Goldman Sachs over the last couple of years! So I did a quick renovation on that, sold that and that then allowed me to have a sizeable pot of cash. I won't hide that, I had a sizeable pot of cash to then go shopping for property in London.

I soon realised that there were all these HMOs or houses of multiple occupancy in Hackney that were just in a dreadful state and yet people wanted homes in the area, particularly luxury homes. So what I started doing is buying HMOs, converting them back into luxury homes and then selling those on.

So converting HMOs back to single family homes?

Yes, single-family homes.

Interesting, that's the reverse strategy to what a lot of people have been doing. But it sounds like you were going upmarket and adding a lot of value in terms of interior design and features?

Yes definitely and just making them really, really luxurious, making them smart homes, putting in underfloor heating, bringing them to a really high standard.

So did that then became a strategy that you just cookie-cuttered and repeated a few times in the same area?

Yes it worked while the markets were going crazy, so in 2012-14, it worked really, really well. Too many people cottoned onto it in 2015 and 2016 and there were too many people coming into the market, so it didn't work so well then. But again, I was really fortunate at that time in 2013 to meet my business partner and that opened a whole new chapter of property forming.

So you've now got your teeth into property, it looks like you've discovered your passion and you've got a handful now of decent projects behind you. What changed when you met this business partner, what was he able to bring to the party?

I had no idea really about property *per se*, I knew what I had done and I knew what was working on those, but he had 30 years of experience. He was used to building boutique smaller developments, up to say 50 flats, that sort of size, and he had his own in-house construction team. I was able to then piggyback off his experience and jump into some of his projects and really learn about how to do projects other than flat-to-house conversions, house-to-flat conversions, that sort of thing. It really did open up my eyes to building, to properly developing projects.

I imagine becoming a property developer was a big transition and therefore you could start getting the scale and the multiple units on each project to give you the size of portfolio that you now have?

Exactly, and I always say to people that it's as much headache doing a single flat as it is doing 50 flats, it's just there are a few more zeros at the end of the numbers. You've got the same planning challenges, the same finance challenges, the same construction, it even takes the same amount of time, you're just doing one flat versus 50.

The only difference I guess is it just needs that larger pot of capital at the start of the project?

Yes it does and more consultants and more surveyors. You need your M&Es (*mechanical and electrical – GR*) and an array of surveyors and you need builders that have got the skill to do those larger type of developments.

So Nicole you managed to build a significant property empire during those boom years of 2012-2014. And now I think we need to talk about the change in market sentiment that's happened in the last couple of years. What are some of the big differences that you're now seeing that are making this a bit more challenging?

We've just had this perfect storm of changes that really turned sentiment away from property and definitely made it more challenging for investors and developers. We had the Stamp Duty changes, we had the Section 24 changes for landlords and then we had the Brexit vote. These things really did cause a lot of uncertainly within the markets and really changed things for us.

So as a result of that, developers are facing planning challenges because planning departments can't staff their planning team properly any more, they just don't have the budgets for that, so planning is taking a lot longer.

Lenders are really clamping down on their criteria and it's much, much harder to secure finance, especially from the High Street banks. It can sometimes take 12 months to secure development finance and even then you don't know if you're going to get it. You can't bank on that – no pun intended!

And then the final thing is properties are not selling. We've had properties on the market now for 12 months - one particular property that's just not sold or had a single offer in that time. The average time on the market now is around 9 months in certain parts of London and I would say that's going to stretch up to closer to 12 and even 24 months as people are just not looking to buy and there's no supply out there.

So these things have really started to put some pressure on developers, including myself.

And certainly I think for me one of the biggest changes, and it's only just starting to be seen by a lot of people, is Section 24. I gave a talk recently at a property investor show, I had about 65 people in the room who were all presumably interested in or active property investors because of where they were, and I said 'how many of you have heard of Section 24?' and there were something like three hands went up.

The impact it's having is massive and yet all around this conference the same gurus were selling this 'get rich in real estate' stuff that may have worked ten years ago, but certainly wouldn't work in this market. What changes are you having to make to your strategy to try and cope with this perfect storm?

Just on your point about Section 24, I think it's interesting that this April I believe will be the first time that these landlords, who are unaware of the changes, are going to be hit with their tax bills, so this is going to cause further ripples in the market.

Fortunately for me, when I first set up my portfolio, I was advised very well, which is why it's always important to get very good advice. My properties are all within corporate structures so I'm not impacted by Section 24 directly, but obviously indirectly I am with the changing feel of the market.

But definitely for me, it's the difficulty selling that I'm finding the most challenging because my strategy has always been buy–renovate–sell, and now I'm not able to sell so I'm having to refinance out and rent out. And that was never my strategy, but now it has had to become my strategy.

Right so it's much more of a buy and hold for the rent roll but I guess that would make you typically tend to want to buy different kinds of property if you were going in with that strategy?

That's right, you don't want luxury prime property because the yield on that is negligible, its 1-2% and in real terms, when you factor in inflation, you're not even covering your costs, often you're not even covering interest costs.

So is it time now to take these luxury properties and turn them back to HMOs?!

Perhaps it is, perhaps it is! We're doing things like short lets, which generally are higher yielding but for me right now with these types of properties it's about just covering interest costs and just biding our time really and waiting until the market changes, until perhaps we get a decision on whether we're in or out with Brexit. And I think, for me my view is that it doesn't matter what the decision is, we just need a decision now and as soon as we have a decision we can plan our lives, then the property market will stabilise.

I think its also worth saying that the impact on a lot of landlords, or we might call them more accidental landlords, is going to be quite a long and a significant one because I just came back from a conference in Prague where I learned that overseas investors are buying up whole swathes of British property from distressed landlords and that distress has come from Section 24. So suddenly there's all this property on the market that is in turn potentially even causing homelessness because there's people now who've not got anywhere to live because landlords are coming out of the rental market.

Yes definitely and I'm seeing that on the developer side. Just last week I had three developers come to me who were distressed. Their bank valuations have come in much lower, which means the banks are pulling their finance. One gentleman unfortunately is about to lose his home and it's really distressing. Some people say 'well these people shouldn't have over-stretched themselves in the first place, they shouldn't have put their homes up as collateral for these loans', but when markets are going up you lose sight of the fact that you can lose your home and these personal guarantees you sign can be enforced. People lose sight of that and it's really difficult not to feel emotional towards these people.

So for me, one new business that I'm looking at setting up is a fund so that we can assist these distressed developers and at least help them save their homes and provide a return for our investors and build out some of these distressed developments.

And what do you see as the impact of these factors you've mentioned on the increasing amount of property crowd funding that's going on through various platforms? There's lots of smaller investors who are now putting in a few thousand because they can't perhaps afford a whole property, but if the market itself is starting to suffer this kind of stagnation and lack of finance, is that going to impact the returns that these crowd funding platforms are going to provide?

Definitely, it's always going to impact investors within these. I think that anyone going into crowd funding has to realise that this is property; this is not sticking your money in a bank account and getting a fixed rate of return, it's higher risk and therefore higher return. A lot of people see the returns advertised as 20%, 25%, 30% guided by the developers and think that that is the return they're going to get but it's not. These are indicative returns and you can lose your money, you can lose all of it and people need to be aware of that.

I think though with crowd funding it's a very good way for people with as little as £500 to get some exposure into property and perhaps hedge themselves against property markets when they do start rising. You look at a lot of developers and they made their money in the downturns. So I do believe that now isn't such a bad time to get into property and go against that tide, when everyone else is selling you buy, that's the whole Warren Buffet idea.

Yes exactly.

And so it's not such a bad idea to start looking at buying property, especially if it's distressed and it's inexpensive.

Okay, so you've been on this amazing journey in the last eight or nine years, from what you've been through what would be one or two golden nougats you'd want to pass onto other people thinking about getting into property investment?

Two things that I'd pass on, number one is 'cash is king' and as property developers are optimistic, we're gamblers as well, we always think that our deal is going to turn to gold and it doesn't. Hold back cash and I would recommend holding back 20-25% of the GDV (*gross development value, i.e.*

the selling price of all the properties in the development added together - GR) of whatever you're working on, hold that back as cash because you're going to need it, you always do. Developers always run out of cash and you'll be in such a strong position if you do hold back that cash, that's number one.

And number two is don't be afraid to collaborate with people and joint venture, because for me I would never have experienced the journey that I've had if I had not taken that plunge and worked with someone who has significantly more experience than I have. It will help your career if you can spread the risk, allocate your funds and your experience and your time among maybe one or two people who are more experienced than you.

Okay and the final question for you is what next for Nicole Bremner?

Yes well it's interesting. As I said I'm looking at setting up this fund so that we can help some distressed developers, it's a recovery fund, that's really interesting. I think a lot of property developers don't look at their cash flow, they don't have a financial director within their company, they can't afford that, so that's another avenue that I'm exploring.

And finally, I'm looking at investing outside of property, I've bought a women's active wear label, I've got a property auction company, I'm looking at a music merchandise company, all these different things that will help me diversify. Because for me property was everything. I was invested heavily in property with just a small amount of shares within my pension and that to me is not a balanced portfolio, so I'm going to go back to my financial planning roots and just reallocating my funds a little more and just be a little more conservative.

Which brings us full circle. Thank you very much indeed Nicole Bremner.

Thank you.

Three Key Lessons
From Nicole Bremner

1. **Know your numbers** – Nicole used her financial background to model the details of her property projects and managed the budgets day to day to keep everything on track. So many business owners and investors are sloppy when it comes to forecasting, monitoring and managing the key metrics that mean the difference between success and failure.

2. **Cash is king** – linked to point 1, and the most common cause of failure for property investors who grow into property developers. As a rule of thumb Nicole suggests keeping 25% of the overall value of the project in free cash as costs always increase and timescales always lengthen.

3. **Be ready to change your strategy when the market turns** – Nicole was one of the first to see the potential to convert tired HMOs into luxury family homes. When that strategy became crowded she moved to developing and selling flats on a large scale. With the slow sales market she is now pivoting again to a buy and hold rental strategy.

Dan Bradbury

Dan Bradbury

Bouncing Back from Near Fatal Injury

Dan Bradbury's career has been nothing if not varied and unique. Starting as a professional squash player, achieving early business success and failure then, just as he was getting on top of things, a near fatal accident.

He's bounced back from that to become a sought-after business coach and a highly successful investor in business turnarounds. Some of Dan's accomplishments:

Age 22: the 3rd fastest reader in the world (The Mind Sports Olympiad)

Age 22: launched my first company, Dreamlife Technology

Age 26: launched my second company, Dan Bradbury Ltd. Was a mid-six figure company in its first year and increased annual revenue to £3.2 million in less than two years.

Mid-20s: started buying distressed companies with the intent of brokering

Age 29: sold my first business for over $1M (Business Growth Systems, Ltd.)

2008: was awarded The Ultimate Marketer by Infusionsoft

2014: acquired a distressed company, turned it around and sold it for $4.3M.

My guest in this chapter is someone who has experienced the ups and downs of the entrepreneurial life from a very early age, including having to recover from a life threatening injury. He is the business coach and serial entrepreneur, Dan Bradbury. Dan welcome to Money & Me.

Thanks for having me Graham, glad to be here.

In a moment I want to come to your business career, which is a really fascinating one, but before we do that I want to take you back in time to your family when you were growing up. Tell me about what your parents did, did they talk to you about money or business or any of these things as you were a kid?

My family is very traditional in many ways but unique in some as well. Both my parents were working class, but over the course of their lives they worked their way up to middle class, I guess you would categorise it as that. My dad, after finishing school he joined the navy briefly. And after he left the navy, he was there only a short space of time, he was deciding what to do for a job and at the time the economy was very uncertain. So he went to his father, who was a working class man, a metalworker, and said well I've got this job or that job, what should I do? One of them was with, what was then, Midland Bank, and my grandfather's advice was they won't go bust so go with them! So my dad promptly joined Midland Bank and worked with them for his entire career, 40+ years.

Consequently it was a very conservative financial household. My parents never really had any debt other than a mortgage, worked hard, saved hard - very traditional. But what was interesting is that I've got one sister and we were almost polar opposites when it came to money. When it came to pocket money time my sister would put it in her savings in her piggy bank and I would promptly go out and spend it and so it continued on that path. I think what's interesting for me is that despite what people would say was good, common sense advice, 'get a job, save hard and buy a house', it didn't' work for me.

It was only when I got a bit older and other experiences I had in my late teens and onwards, that really shifted my belief about money. When I was in my early teens, I'd say I'm not untypical in that, you don't listen to your parents, or

I certainly didn't. So I didn't follow the advice, I was just spending everything I earned and that's why I'm quite fanatical about financial education these days and for my children and I believe it should be taught in schools because yeah, parents giving you the advice is not always listened to…

It's interesting to have a banker for a father you'd think that perhaps they would imbue a bit of a saving discipline but it just comes down to personality in the end doesn't it? Were you a little bit of a rebel do you think, would that be a fair comment?

Yes maybe, I think classically entrepreneurial or you could just say a teenage boy in that I aspired to have nice things, nice clothes. When I was old enough to drive I wanted to have a nice car, which is just normal. And then in today's consumer mad age, especially when I was growing up, it was the relative birth of the internet, consumerism just exploded even more, so then I remember I was waiting for my 18th birthday for two reasons. One thing was my mum had faithfully put some money every month into a savings account that I could get access to when I was 18. So I literally got that money out, went into the bank, because I was told I could get a £500 overdraft when I was 18, and promptly went and got that overdraft and within two weeks had blown the lot.

Well that was a great start, but I think you did have a rather unconventional career choice at that point didn't you?

Yes, so my passion was squash, I played to a reasonably high standard and it's not the most profitable of careers, but I wanted to be a professional squash player. I probably could have gone on to university, and that was certainly my parents' strong encouragement. My sister, by contrast, went on to be a vet, and I said do you know what, I really want to do this and I was doing squash coaching, teaching kids and adults squash in order to make ends meet really.

And it was only when that career ended because I had some injury problems and I realised it wasn't going to work, that I got into a position where I realised I needed to do something about this. I met a girl that I really liked, wanted to take her out for a drink but I realised I literally had no money. I remember scratching down the back of my parents' sofa trying to find the £5 to £10 so I could take her out for a drink and I went 'yeah, I need to address this money thing!'

Right but it's a huge leap from that, which a lot of people can identify with, I've got no money, but to then say well the answer is I'm going to start a business. That's not the conclusion a lot of people come to, a lot of people just go out and get a job.

So what was that spark of an idea that said I actually want to go and do my own thing in business?

Well it was two things, one was desire, because the girl that I met had an extremely famous and wealthy father and that inspired me to want to have greater things in life. And then simultaneously, a friend from the tennis and squash club where I trained, was my age and yet he'd somehow – I still don't know how, I don't think he knows how – managed to get a very lucrative job, so aged 19 he was making six figures a year. He was a consultant working for a large consultancy firm and we got talking and we were just bouncing off each other and I said well how have you done that, and he said well its easy, you just go and you help people and you solve problems. We kind of just wound each other up and ended up saying 'look, let's set up a business'.

I had a passion, an interest in personal development because I believe, probably from my parents, that whilst I didn't get on with mainstream education that if you can learn things you can make life better, and you can learn pretty much anything. So I got into personal development and got into accelerated learning techniques. I became very adept at memory techniques and speed reading skills and suddenly it became obvious to me. Tim then became my business partner and we said let's start this accelerated learning company, let's teach these techniques in schools and that was the genesis of the business idea.

And you were what, 22 at the time?

I think I was 20, I think that business started when I was about 19/20 years old.

Oh wow.

Yes and we had huge aspirations and we had a great product, so I'd gotten so obsessed with speed reading – believe it or not there's actually a speed reading world championships Graham.

It's not quite as glamorous as it sounds, not that it sounds glamorous, but I entered it and the first year I came sixth and the next year I came third. So technically, it's not a widely competed tournament, but technically I was the third fastest reader in the world.

A bronze medal then.

Indeed, a bronze medallist, and so we had a great product. Yet, in a relatively short space of time, we racked up a ton of debt because back at that time, which was the early 2000s, you pretty much just had to go to a bank and say can I have a loan please and they'd say what's it for, and you'd say well I'm going to do a business and they would just go yeah, here you go. So despite not having a job and being 20 I managed to rack up over £100,000 worth of unsecured consumer debt trying to make a business work. But the lesson I suppose in hindsight was, the product wasn't the problem, it's that I didn't' know how to market and sell, I didn't know how to make money. So ultimately the business folded and I was left licking my wounds.

Oh wow, but I think its quite often that process and the lessons you learn from it that put you in a really good position the next time around and I think it wasn't long after that that you launched another business with a bit more success?

Yes exactly right. I recognise the importance of mentoring and you know the girl's famous father was Eric Clapton and he would talk about the people that inspired him musically and how he learned and how he developed. And I was smart enough to figure out, look I can declare bankruptcy and go and get a job, but that's not going to give me what I want from a lifestyle, from a career perspective, I need to learn how to add more value.

And I recognised that I didn't know how to market and sell. So I went and got the only 'proper' job I've ever had working in sales for a training company. Tt had the advantage of getting me trained in sales skills but also it was NLP and personal development stuff, so I also got to subsidise my desire for more training. I was in the right place at the right time and my early mentor, a guy called Andy, said to me, if you do what I tell you to Dan, by the end of the year you'll be making £100,000 a year. And I believed him.

Now I don't know whether he believed it or not but it didn't matter, I was on that treadmill and I relentlessly applied what he told me and went back and made phone calls and he listened in and he gave me feedback and ultimately I learned to sell. The company grew and as the company grew I got into marketing and by the age of 22 I had a £40,000 a month marketing budget to spend and I was making six figures a year.

So Dan, how did that second business go based on all this new knowledge you'd learned?

It just took off. Because I'd acquired the skills, the marketing and sales particularly, I was able to add value and started consistently making more money and over the next 4, 5, 6 years had one business, got that up and running, got a second business up and running, got a third business up and running and by most people's accounts, you would say I was very successful and making a lot of money because I had businesses that were printing cash. So it felt quite good for a while.

But of course, these things don't always last and in your case it was something totally out of left field that happened when you decided to do an Ironman event, tell me the story of what happened.

I had gotten into doing triathlons and I was in an Ironman triathlon and I was coming down a hill on my bike when my tyre burst and I was thrown head first into a tree. I hit the tree so hard that my helmet split and ultimately I ended up with a brain injury - similar, but thankfully for me, not as serious as what happened to Michael Schumacher with his skiing accident. I was in a coma and ultimately, when I came round, it took many months to recover full cognitive function.

And for a period the doctors were advising my family, you know he may not recover, he might stay like this. I couldn't concentrate for more than a minute or two so even reading was difficult because I'd lose concentration every sentence or couple of sentences.

And that's when I had a real epiphany, I looked back and I went, holy crap, if I don't regain my ability to earn, even though I was lucky that I'd cleared my debt and I had had high income and we had some money, my family weren't set for life. I had two young children and I realised I've been a higher income earner for nearly a decade, but in real terms it wouldn't have kept us going for more than a couple of years before my wife would have had to have gone back to work to support the family. And that's when I realised it had to change.

So I guess you still had some of those habits you had as a teenager, where it was easy come, easy go with the money and you were what they call 'high income, under invested?'

That's exactly right. I think there's a difference between making money and keeping it and I think I'd learned to make money but I hadn't learned to keep it. So the starter for me was that I had three businesses at that point so I took one of them that I felt was most exitable and I decided to sell this to kick-start my investment pot. To take a chunk of money off the table to clear the mortgage and have some money to fund more passive or ongoing investment cash flow sources. But the problem was I didn't know how to do it!

But fortunately I knew I could find a mentor or somebody that can teach me that. I found two people that had done big eight figure exits and got some advice from them and within a year of my injury I did my first deal; I exited that business for a seven figure sum, which sounds great but actually it was even better than that because, frankly, at the time of the injury, it probably wasn't worth a six figure sum.

So by learning the skills about how I exited my own business, I actually bought another company and merged the two together and that kick-started me down the mergers and acquisitions route.

I guess you being the front man of all these businesses running around doing all the work and suddenly now you're in a hospital bed unable to focus for very long, that must have made you think I need some kind of businesses or some kind of income where I'm not the one doing all the work and I have to become more of the investor and the owner rather than the operator?

Exactly, I had been an owner/operator owner, and I think that I learned that I couldn't out-earn my spending desires and I needed to invest in assets. Actually, when I looked at it, all the people that had really made money were people that were owners not operators. And so they owned businesses and they'd either made money through exiting and selling or they built one business up, removed themselves from it, maintained the cash flow and then went and built subsequent businesses.

You know if you are the operator you've got a job, it might be a very highly paid job and there's nothing wrong with that, but it certainly doesn't create the level of autonomy and financial freedom that I craved. So gradually in the years since then, I got more and more into mergers and acquisitions and into private equity and just seeing businesses as investment vehicles, as assets.

So when you buy a business, you merge it or turn it around, you sell it, what are you then doing with the proceeds to invest in longer-term assets? Are you taking money off the table and investing in something else?

Yes I'm a fan of diversification, I think that while my income comes from the businesses, whether exits or the cash flow dividends from those businesses, I would deem that to be very high risk. I learned, because of the injury, as a classic entrepreneur I was immune to risk until it happened to me! Now, I take as much of the money, not all the money, that I can off the table and put it into the most, what I would say, boring investment. It goes in low cost index trackers, so I'm in the Stock Market, I'm in property where it is much more time leveraged and passive. The returns are inferior but it's much more stable. The idea being that there is a hard asset base but actually it's the cash flow that is produced from that, which means that if I decide to go and throw myself at a tree again, you know there's cash flow for the time to come.

I've heard it described as fast pounds in business versus slow pounds in an investment portfolio (see James Sinclair interview – GR) and in a sense the business is there to generate the fast pounds that you then transfer into the slow pounds that give you that longer term security.

Yes I like that, I haven't heard it described that way, but yes that's my sentiment entirely. One of my friends and a long time mentor, who is worth £100+ million describes it as getting rich is boring. His advice to me is that it's important to get people that balance you out. I'm entrepreneurial and young, and he's in his late 60s now, he says 'Dan, just calm down', because I had to be entrepreneurial and try things in order to get some traction but as I've built more wealth I've become more conservative because there's been more to lose.

So it's been more about risk mitigation and about okay how do you now protect this and preserve this because you know I think Warren Buffett is right, compounded growth being the eighth wonder of the world or whatever the phrase is, it's sometimes the biggest wins are the losses avoided.

That's why, if I take a high-risk venture, great, it can be very lucrative. How can I mitigate the downside investment in that but then how can I take as much of that money off the table and get it into long term stable solid investments because that's the platform which frees you up mentally to do all this stuff? It's the investor mindset, which you can't do if you're scrabbling around robbing Peter to pay Paul, rich one month and devastated the next.

And I guess the other side of what you're doing now is that you can go for bigger and bigger and bigger transactions and is there an element of having to almost recalibrate your thinking to say that I could pull together these seven or eight figure enterprises and make a significant exit and liquidity event from that process?

Yes there is. I think it's interesting because I've gotten more conservative. At one point, when I did a seven figure exit that I mentioned, immediately I was thinking oh I want an eight figure exit and I subsequently did do a much bigger deal than my first. I've got a friend who runs a TV channel funnily enough, I won't mention it, this is the TV channel you should be watching, but he exited a business of his last year for £85 million. But what's interesting is, and we've spoken a lot about it, is he's much more into having multiple sources of income.

So while I might look at the whole pot and aggregate businesses together in the same sector, I'm in favour of diversified asset classes and there's some strength in that diversity. So on paper I might look at each opportunity from a net worth point of view, I'm a fan of measuring it collectively – they are separate entities although there can be significant accretive advantage from merging a couple of businesses together. But, at this stage, I'm not a fan of putting all my eggs in one basket on the basis that I think everybody watching or reading this can name multiple people that have made money once and lost it. I think the aim of the game is to get rich and stay rich!

And so yeah, I'm a fan of diversification and that builds a platform for growth. But you are correct, as the transaction sizes get bigger; it's actually the same game. In fact a friend of mine called Peter, who was another early guide for me, at one time I heard him do a particular deal where he made a lot of money and I looked at it and, I don't remember the amounts because it was a long time ago, but it was a mind blowing amount of money for me at the time. And I said 'Peter, I know you're a smart guy, how did you make so much money so easily?' He said 'Dan, the only difference between you and I is I put an extra couple of zeros at the end of my invoices'.

I think that's why I'm fanatical about surrounding myself with people and trying to stretch my thinking because ultimately, you've got to get your head round this stuff. I think it is an environment you have to immerse yourself in, you need to watch programmes like this and study it because it takes time, but actually, as you learn it, there's not much difference between this level and this higher level, it's just the same fundamentals practiced at more depth. And then ultimately that makes the difference between a negligible net worth and an extremely high one.

Fantastic. Well it sounds like in a way that that period that you had recovering from that injury has been transformational in terms of your thinking and the results you've achieved, that's phenomenal. Dan Bradbury thanks very much for sharing that with us.

Thanks for having me Graham.

Three Key Lessons
From Dan Bradbury

1. **Marketing and sales are vital business skills.** It doesn't matter how great your idea is or how good your product, if you don't know how to market or sell your products and services your business is going to struggle. I remember meeting Dan at several American events where we'd each paid thousands of dollars to learn the latest techniques so we could apply them to our businesses.

2. **Create wealth in business then invest it.** Similar to James Sinclair's approach with fast pounds and slow pounds, Dan uses his businesses to generate rapid profits then takes money off the table into investments like tracker funds and property. Done right, real wealth creation can be 'boring' but predictable, especially when you add in the power of compounding.

3. **Be ready to deal with life's shocks.** His near fatal cycling accident forced Dan to re-think his entire business strategy and set him on the road to the success he enjoys today. Are you the lynchpin of your business? What would happen if you were unable to work for months on end? Take a look at how your business and your investment portfolio is structured and try to create passive income that does not demand your presence.

Siam Kidd

Siam Kidd

From RAF Pilot To Crypto and Currency Trader

Siam is an ex-RAF Pilot turned full time investor, business owner and financial markets trader.

Siam has accurately forecasted many major economic events. He grew his account by 30% during the Swiss Franc unpegging from the Euro in Jan 2015, he grew his Trading fund in 2015 by 60% and made £422k in one day for during the Black Monday crash of 2015. More recently, in 2017 helped his 700 private Crypto Investing students make over £3m in combined profits and then navigated them to growing their token holdings by over 300% during the 90% fall/bear market of 2018 and 2019.

Since 2015, Siam has been active in the Mergers & Acquisitions area growing a small Group of companies.

Sickened with the fact that the internet is full of scams and unethical companies that teach 'Day Trading', he founded The Realistic Trader and mentors people on how to properly trade using sound risk management and trading methods. He also texts out to his students every trade he places in real time which has been a great success since he started this in 2013.

Learn more at therealistictrader.com

My guest in this chapter has been an RAF pilot, a precious metals trader, a Forex trader and now a cryptocurrency expert helping other people to make money in the financial markets. His name is Siam Kidd. Siam welcome to Money & Me.

Hello, thank you.

So let's go back a few years to your childhood growing up. Tell me a bit about your family environment and whether things like money or investing ever kind of got discussed.

So my dad is English, my mum is Thai and they set up East Anglia's first Thai restaurant like donkeys years ago. And I guess, because my mum's Thai, the Thai culture is very hard working, like everyone in Thailand you're pretty much born into poverty and so I was child slave labour from the age of I guess 5 until 18!

In the restaurant?

Yes I was watching the restaurant and as soon as I was presentable I was a waiter, for free.

I guess working in a family business environment must have helped you get some sense of what was involved in running a business?

I learned the fact that the business owner, i.e. my mum and dad, had to do everything. I don't think they knew much about delegation. We had staff but their attitude was 'if it's got to be done right you've got to do it yourself' etc, and I think the key thing they instilled in me is that you really have to work hard with whatever you're doing. But it was only when I was older that I realised you have to work smart and hard, not just hard.

Indeed. So, as you were growing up, was the concept of money and investing for the future discussed at all?

No, literally 'money doesn't grow on trees' and 'we're trying to send you to the best school we can' blah, blah, blah. So nothing about investing, my parents never invested and as such I was probably the most degenerate money person on the planet until I was about 24.

Okay! So your first career venture was to go into the RAF as a pilot. What was the motivation behind that?

From the age of 8 I'd always wanted to be a pilot. So when I was about 8 my parents had a bit of a financial hiccup and we lived in a nice house and we had to move out and we moved into the smallest apartment ever, like every corridor an 8 year old could touch both sides.

Deceptively spacious.

Yeah. And I think he had trouble selling the house because it was quite a large house and he ended up renting it to two RAF Jaguar pilots out of RAF Coltishall. He just kept on bigging them up going 'ah they have brains the size of computers' and then Top Gun came out in the late 1980s/90s and he was saying 'oh God these are amazing'. I managed to meet them once and because he had idolised them so much I was thinking 'oh you guys are Gods'. So I think that sort of helped.

It's quite a rigorous selection process get into the RAF isn't it?

Yes, I basically spent my whole childhood from 8 to 18 trying to become a pilot, to the point where all of my friends called me Space Cadet because I was an Air Force cadet and all that sort of stuff. And then I just did everything. I got my pilot's licence before my driving licence, so when I was 16/17 I got that and got loads of flying scholarships and then managed to get in. Because I'm not clever - I got two Ds for my A-Levels!

Wow, and did it live up to your expectations, did you enjoy it as much as you hoped you would?

Yes and no. The aircraft, amazing, the people, amazing but like with any big beast of an organisation there's so much red tape and bureaucracy. Joining the Air Force was the best thing I've ever done in my life, leaving the Air Force was the second best thing.

Okay, and was there a specific thing you left the Air Force to do? Did you have a plan in mind?

Yes, I left for ignoble reasons, basically I needed more money. I joined the Air Force when I was 18 and I started trading when I was 18. For the first four years I was literally the worst trader ever, I lost £100,000 in my first four years basically.

Ouch.

Yeah, I had this system where I was taking home about £2,200 a month in salary, I blew £2,000 a month on the markets and spent £200 on partying and booze. So that was my system for four years. I didn't know why I kept losing!

Yet something obviously happened because the losing stopped.

Yes, basically if you treat anything like a hobby you'll get hobby-like results, whereas if you treat something like a business you'll get businesslike results. So I was basically spraying and praying, placing any old trades, chasing trades in the markets and getting nowhere and I wasn't taking any notes or doing any trading bookkeeping so to speak. And first of all that is the biggest secret in trading, like if you're a business owner, if you don't know your key stats like your turnover, your net and gross margin and your opex etc, you're going to fail and it's the same with trading.

Okay, so you turned it into more of a businesslike approach and then you started making money from it and then at some point you decide it's successful enough as a system you can teach others?

I had ups and downs, so I think when I was about 23 I had my first big win. I was this cocky little 23 year old pilot driving around base in an Aston Martin, which I cringe reminiscing back, but I think I lulled myself into a false sense of security because I had a six month winning streak and I thought I'm Billy Big Balls here, and yeah, that went wrong. So I then lost it all - I kept the Aston though!

Hard assets, good.

Yes. Once I started doing things properly I was consistent and then I left the Air Force.

So you got to that consistent point and then you started teaching others. Now what have you found as being the difference between say your most successful pupils and the ones that don't make it?

It's interesting because I thought the more academic person would be better, it turns out they're the worst. I've trained thousands and thousands of traders and the less academic people are by far the best. One of our best students was a car mechanic, a body repair mechanic, and he was just said 'right, this is all new to me, I'll just do what you say Siam, I'll just learn everything'. And he didn't break any rules, he did proper logging and the thing is you can only get better with trading if you have your stats, i.e., if you log and he did that perfectly, he didn't break any rules. And within a two year period, as much as I hate to admit it, he was as good as me.

This is all about compliance isn't it because the academics presumably over-thought it and reckoned that they could do something better?

Yes they would say 'I've got degrees in statistics, who is this Muppet over here?' They tried to reengineer everything and over-think things.

I can imagine.

One of the key things that I see most people failing on is that on a chart you can lay indicators, so moving averages, Bollinger Bands, all that sort of stuff and what people try and do is they put ten indicators on or five different indicators, they're all squiggly lines, it makes the chart a mess and it's conflicting signals. They're trying to get that Swiss cheese alignment, where right, everything's aligned, now place a trade. But by the time everything is aligned the trade has already gone!

Right, so you have to keep it relatively simple but have a clear view of what you're looking for. Because one of the things I've seen that I think is concerning, is when people look on trading as a get rich quick scheme and they think they can just come into it and immediately start making some money without any training and I think the statistics are against them.

Yes, there's the 90-90-90 rule - 90% of people lose 90% of their capital in the first 90 days.

Wow!

It's nuts. Pretty much everyone loses and it's due to how the system is geared up. You have the brokers, basically the ones that make real money are the brokers, the exchangers. And what happens is they give out affiliate links to people to send new traders to their thing. What they do is they'll go to a trading educator and go 'hey, for every person you send over we'll give you a kickback of their trading commission up to 40%'. And so what happens is that this trading educator, they tend to be low on morals, they then teach day trading, which in a nutshell is a form of high-paced trading where you're placing lots of highly leveraged trades all of the time. That just generates so many fees for the broker and then the educator gets the kickback.

Yes and the person doing the trading loses their money and it's a bit of a sorry mess.

The exchangers say 'oh no, it's in our best interests if we have really successful traders', which does make sense, but really the exchangers, all they need is a break even trader, because if you're a break even trader, especially a break even day trader, you're placing really highly leveraged bets and quite a lot of them so you're generating loads of fees. But, because let's say I'm a break even day trader, because I'm not losing my capital I'm going to keep on trading.

Okay, so if somebody is reading this and thinking that they want to get started in financial trading, how can we position their expectations as to how long a process like this should take?

Its definitely a life skill, you're not going to learn overnight - I would budget in your head 5-10 years.

5-10 years?

Yes and that's the ugly truth that no one likes to hear. They say 'oh I'm not going to wait 5-10 years to get good at it', and then they go and end up day trading with one of these educators.

Right, I guess what you're also saying is that if they go through a proper training programme you can maybe short circuit that somewhat and certainly avoid the big losses that can come early on?

It's basically a 5-10 year play, which most people don't like to hear, they want the £2,000 a month from day one and that's not going to happen. It took me six years to get consistently profitable. You can skip things, it takes maybe 2 years till you're consistently profitable, but it's a bit like medicine. Any doctors watching this, they're going to cringe but there are far more surgeons on the planet than successful traders on the planet. Doing a 2 day trading course and expecting to be good on the markets is like trying to perform surgery after a 2 day training course.

But people always want the easy button don't they and to be fair, often times it's marketed as get rich quick - you have the guy by the pool with his Ferrari on the drive, look what I've done, you could do this in the next few weeks...

Yeah.

That's pretty much the promise isn't it, which is just not the truth.

And in fact with all those people you see, the main profits that they've made are from business not from trading.

Yes.

And I've experienced this first hand because when I left the Air Force and I was full time trading, I tried to live off my trading account and it was incredibly hard and frustrating because you'd make all the profit then you'd have to go and pay your rent and utility bills and so your capital never really grows. Then I started setting up businesses and, once my lifestyle was being covered by my businesses and I just left my account just to bumble along, that's when the real profits came.

And then we're getting the compounding effect as well of course.

Exactly.

Which is where some of the real wealth comes from.

Yes. And I guess it's also a life skill because pretty much once a decade we'll have a global crash of some sort, it could be in any asset. If you know how to trade you can short that and profit from it.

As the markets come down.

Yeah and that's where I make all of my profits.

Okay, so it sounds like what we're saying is trading needs to be treated as a part time business.

Yes.

So it's a business, it's not a hobby, but you need another form of income that keeps you going so you're not going to put too much strain either on your capital or on your trading mindset during those early years.

Yes 100%.

Okay brilliant. Now I want to turn to another hot topic in the trading world and that's cryptocurrencies. Siam obviously we've been way up into the sky with Bitcoin and we've come crashing back to earth, what's your analysis of what's been going on in the crypto market?

Where do I start? The thing I tend to say is that cryptos are the evolution of money and Distribution Ledger Technologies (DLT) Blockchain is the revolution of trust. So lets look at the money bit. We've had a few evolutions in money, we've moved from bartering to coined money 2,400 years ago in Lydia, and then we went from coined money to digital money in the 1960s and 70s and we're now going from digital money to cryptocurrency or crypto money, more currency than anything. And so it's just a natural evolution.

Cryptos are a digital currency governed and secured by cryptography, which makes it quite secure, but its peer-to-peer, that's the key thing. I can send money from my wallet to your wallet, no middlemen banks in the way.

So it's evolutionary or even revolutionary in that change, but also of course I suppose this causes the existing banks and governments to think 'ooh what's going on here; we can't control this', so there's been something of a backlash from the powers that be.

Yes, so the one thing that the whole industry is worried about is that it's completely unregulated. The key driver of the 2017 bull run was because you could have a teenager in his bedroom creating a white paper and then raising millions off the back of that with no product, no idea, no team, nothing. So the year of the ICO (*initial coin offering – GR*) is gone, like that's so 2017.

It's the initial coin offering, where somebody launched a new cryptocurrency overnight from their bedroom.

Exactly, it was a bit like the internet, where people were raising millions for websites which didn't exist or couldn't exist etc. So now what's happening is that regulation is being stamped onto the market so we're going to have Security Token Offerings (STOs), so more of the same but it's more established and the big boys are coming in.

And do you think that will see the revival of price movements in the crypto market?

Most definitely yes; though most of it again is going to be hype. I'm a big fan of cryptos but I'm also its biggest critic as well, so it's 99% hype, BS and just rubbish and fake news and 1% utility value. There's just 1% of the market that is actually doing something in the real world. But contrary to belief, cryptos are actually going to profit the banks quite considerably. If you look at interbank settlements it's a multi-billion dollar industry, so I can see JP Morgan there and Barclays, if they wanted to send billions to each other cross borders it would take at least three days and cost millions in transaction fees. Whereas there are cryptos now and they're already using a crypto called Ripple - I'm not a fan of it, but they can do the same transaction in 30 seconds with next to zero fees.

Wow!

And the billions in savings is going to go to their bottom line.

I think what's fascinating for me, after initially decrying cryptos; quietly it started being announced last year that some of the banks have actually launched their own trading desks in cryptos.

Oh yes all of them - every big bank has a 'Blockchain innovation department', which is code for 'how the hell do we keep on top of this and make money from it?'

Yes inded.

And you'll see some neutral ground middlemen because if Barclays launches Barclays Coin, JP Morgan is not going to use Barclays Coin are they or HSBC aren't going to use Barclays Coin. So there will be middle ground and I think like Ripple is one of them and a few others will pop up.

Right but once the institutional money comes into the sector that I guess will give it that boost to the market again?

Yes definitely, so if you look at the whole market at the moment it's $0.3 trillion so the total crypto market is $300 billion I think. If you look at gold, gold is $7 trillion, so it's considerably larger than cryptos, but if you look at global stock markets its $70 trillion and the global bond market is $100 trillion.

What tends to happen is when we have say an equity crash of some sort and you see all the news headlines of $6 trillion wiped off stocks or Apple has just lost $500 billion or whatever, it's not wiped off, its simply transferred.

So if we had say an equity crash or a property crash, it's a fair shout to say that a small chunk of it or even a tiny slither of it will fall into cryptos as a hedge against uncertainty, because it's uncorrelated.

And the other topic that raises for me is something that I think is quite a parallel with cryptos and that's precious metals, especially gold, which I know has been an area you have been very active in.

Yes, I love gold.

So what do you see as the current and future state of things like gold which has been somewhat depressed recently compared to what you might have expected?

Gold will always be money, so if you really get into the definitions, the only thing on the planet that is money is gold and silver as in it is the only store of value over a long period of time. Cryptos will never be money because the key thing that separates currency and money is the store of wealth over a long period of time.

But Bitcoin I guess is the closest thing to digital gold as possible, it's a foreign currency for everyone and Obama basically said it's like having a Swiss bank account in your pocket, which is spot on actually.

So at the moment, in terms of your personal investment, would you be putting new money into gold and precious metals today?

No. I guess, as a trader, I'm always looking at ratios, so the seesaw, and if you analyse the historic value of certain assets against certain assets you'll see certain correlations. For example stocks and property are inversely related to gold and silver, they move in 20 year cycles, but what is likely to happen is cryptos are quite likely to move a lot higher and faster before gold and silver. So the plan for me is to make wealth in this very scammy, cruddy market and then extract it and re-diversify into real assets: gold, silver, land, businesses.

But that's phase 2 once you've made the money in the crypto market?

Yes definitely; so the way I see assets is that you have primary, secondary and tertiary assets.

A primary asset is based on something which is real, so let's take copper. If you had a whole bunch of land and there was a copper deposit that would be your primary asset. A secondary asset is if I set up a copper factory and do refining etc, and the tertiary would be if I was a futures trader trading copper futures contracts. If you make loads of money as trader up here its almost like in the wind, there's no real longevity, so the goal is you have higher risk but higher reward up here. Once you make your profits, cryptos are up here as well, you need to accelerate down into the secondary or primary assets.

Okay, then the primary asset is a longer term hold and it's going to throw off income for the long term?

Yes.

We're obviously going through this whole dreaded Brexit process at the moment, is that in any way impacting on or should it impact on our investment strategy?

It depends who you are I guess is the standard consultant answer, it depends. If you're an exporting business yes, it's worth diversifying or re-positioning yourself. As you can see, there are loads of businesses jumping into the UK now and some jumping out, so it depends who you are.

From a trading perspective it's been really quite fun. What I have always said is that the mainstream media are the best contrarian indicators. Recently I took a big buy order in pounds sterling. Everyone thought I was nuts, everyone thought why are you buying the pound with the whole Brexit kerfuffle going on? And what happens is because the media always coax the public into doing the wrong thing at the wrong time, always, throughout history, and the pound has been bashed relentlessly for a couple of months now, so a lot of the news and the anticipated news is already baked into the price. There's no more shorters, there's no one else out there to sell the pound, so I took a big buy position yesterday and it's come off, it's been a nice trade.

I know one of the topics close to your heart is our education system or more specifically, its shortcomings.

Yes!

As you start thinking about your own children and their education what are your plans for them?

It's pleasing to see that there's a bit of an awakening within the education system. I think most people are aware that the system we have right now is based from the Industrial Revolution 220 odd years ago and it hasn't changed - we still have age groups in classes and bells and everything Sir Ken Robinson has spoken about, but it's not geared for the next 20 years. If you look at all the exponential technologies, they are all basically about to hit the vertical part, and what we don't know are the permutations of what the tech is going to do. You could sort of extrapolate what the internet was going to do back in the 1990s and it's branched God knows how many techs, but we're now having ten different techs all about to do what the internet did.

So it's a fair shout to say, even if you look at linear growth, rather than the exponential growth we're experiencing, but even if you looked at linear growth, it's easy to see that 90% of all jobs will be displaced by robotics, AI, 3D printing and nanotech. So all our kids right now are basically being cultivated to become redundant and yes I've got two babies and I don't trust any school to send them to.

So you're going to educate them yourself and then hopefully actually change the education system for the better?

Yes I'm building my own school, which won't have a syllabus - we're just questioning a lot of things which should be questioned.

Well I think we'll have to have another conversation about that another time.

Yes indeed!

For now, Siam Kidd, thank you very much indeed.

Thank you.

Three Key Lessons
From Siam Kidd

1. **Treat trading as a business, not a hobby.** If you treat it like a hobby you get hobby results. Treat it like a business by keeping detailed records, logging why you entered trades and what was the outcome. Only by developing this level of discipline and professionalism can you expect to achieve consistent results.

2. **Allow 5-10 years to develop your skills!** Not what you may want to hear, but trading the financial markets is a complex business that needs knowledge, experience and discipline. Remember that 90% of traders lose 90% of their capital in the first 90 days, so if you want to see different results you need to take a different, patient approach.

3. **Don't let the media dictate your strategy.** If anything, treat the mainstream media as a contra-indicator. Much of the negative coverage they specialise in will already be in the price, while markets tend to rise or fall based on a view of future rather than past events. If your market antennae are finely tuned you can go against the crowd and make a killing.

John Howard

John Howard
Bricks & Mortar, Footie & Horses

John is a 40 year veteran of the property sector, during which time he has been involved in the sale and purchase of over 3500 houses, apartments and developments within the UK.

He has built a substantial rental portfolio including houses, hotels and large scheme developments and his experience in running property businesses gives him a unique perspective that he shares on his website and through his coaching programmes. As one of his experienced business partners said, "The advice you get might not be what you want to hear but it is probably right!"

John is actively involved in the Conservative party, has been a football club director and racehorse trainer and now focuses on sharing his industry knowledge through his training company.

John recently captured his property experience in his new book, John Howard's Inside Guide to Property Development and Investment for Newcomers. He frequently appears in TV and the press and speaks at functions and seminars across the country.

Learn more at johnhowardpropertyexpert.co.uk

My guest in this chapter is best known these days as one of our leading property developers, but as you'll find when we go back over his life, he's had lots of different roles and been successful in all of them. His name is John Howard. John welcome to Money & Me.

Thank you.

Now I know you were a very early starter in the property investment game

I was.

That probably had something to do with the kind of family background that you were brought up in?

It did; my father was a greengrocer and then he decided, when I was about 11 years old, to become an estate agent. He was a good greengrocer but obviously everyone knew him as a greengrocer in Felixstowe, not as an estate agent, so they obviously said 'well what do you know about estate agency?', which is a fair question to be honest with you.

I used to hold the tape for him when we were going around measuring up houses; now it's all done with a red light isn't it but in those days you had to hold the tape. In the holidays I also used to cycle round and if I saw a 'For Sale' board I'd get 50p for telling him, and then he'd go and knock on the door and try and get it for sale. So yes I started early!

Then I think eventually on leaving school you went straight into the family firm?

Yes I had to because my father had been very ill and there was virtually no business there really. So I joined him at 17, he then went back into hospital after four months, so I was running the business, very badly by the way, at 17 years and four months with one part-time secretary, not really knowing what I was doing. We had insurance brokers, we had a building society and we did property management and it was a great, great learning curve, and of course we were struggling, we weren't doing very well. So that is a great apprenticeship.

But what changed because I think you trebled the business in a very short time?

What happened was on my 18th birthday I bought two properties off a property developer client we had - it was the end of a deal and they just wanted to get out of it. So I managed to persuade my mother to lend me £2,500, I saved £1,500 and the bank lent me £8,000, I think it was. In those days you'd go to the Bank Manager and he'd actually say yes. So that's what I did and I bought and sold one of them very quickly, I sold it to the sitting tenant, which is always quite a good trick if you could do that in those days, and I moved on.

I always say when I do my seminars, if you're borrowing money from family always make sure they get a good interest rate and they get a share of the profit because guess what, my mother wanted to lend me some more money! So she lent me some more and after two or three deals I didn't need her help anymore, bless her heart – she's still alive at 92 and wants to know what I'm doing. It went on from there and then when I was 19 the business had improved a bit but my father wanted to sell it. We had a buyer who then fell through so then I bought it off him – he didn't want to sell it to me because he didn't want me to fail, which was sweet of him – and I changed the name straight away and then I sold it four years later!

Wow, so that was an apprenticeship in the whole property world.

The very best you could have Graham, the very best.

But then you went off and did something totally different in the football world.

Well what happened was my school report said 'John there's more to life than football', but actually about eight years later I ended up owning part of a professional football club. They weren't quite right, but they were nearly right. I met my main backer, and I still deal with the family now, when I was 24 and we rapidly bought quite a lot of properties and quite successfully. By the time I was 25/26 I had always been a football fan, every football Director is a frustrated footballer and I managed to get involved with Cambridge United and become a Director. At the time I was one of the youngest Directors in the Football League.

For most people, let's face it, once they go into being a Director of a football club it's like digging a great big hole and pouring money into it. Don't tell me you actually made money out of the beautiful game?

No, no, I was there 18 years, had a fantastic time. Four of us really ran the football club and we went from the bottom of the 4th Division to the playoffs for the Premiership, which was an amazing achievement for a club with gates of 5,000 at the most. I had a fantastic time, I learnt a lot because of course when you're in property you only deal with property people, but there I was at 25/26 sitting round a Boardroom table with all different types of businessmen who I had to work with, and that was different for me and it was good for me. And we had a great, great time. We were very disciplined and we never really put very much money in. Once we put the initial capital in we were very disciplined and then 15 years later I bought the ground, which didn't go down very well but I had been there 15 years and the club needed someone to buy the ground and lease it back to them for 50 years, which is what myself and my partner did.

So effectively they got a whole load of capital that they could use to build the team and you became their landlord?

Yes to reduce the debt and all the rest of it and I became the landlord, which was a bit weird having sat there for 15 years and then obviously for the next three years I was the landlord. Things changed and I eventually got ousted off the Board, which was the only time that's ever happened to me. I thought there was something a bit odd when I went into the Board Meeting that night that no one was talking to me and most of the Directors I'd worked with for 15 years had already gone, so I knew something was up.

Isn't there a parallel here between football and politics in that all careers end in failure?

Well I think it's a bit like being a football Manager; you're going to fail at some point.

Indeed - but you continued your property development career during those years?

Oh yes, very much so, yes.

Then I believe you saw the 2007/2008 crash coming, which so many people didn't.

Yes.

What did you see in terms of reading runes?

I've survived three recessions so there's a few tricks, and I say this now and again, one is car sales. When car sales start declining rapidly property normally follows and when car sales start going up it's time to get back in. It's very simple I know and normally it works. At the moment with diesels and so on, it's a bit different probably this time round. But interest rates are incredibly low and like me Graham you remember 10% or 15% interest rates. And some of the developers today don't know they're born to be honest with you.

Indeed.

So yes, over a period of time you know I've bought and sold over 3,500 properties, I've been active all the way through my career. The only thing I have never done is really buy in London, which obviously I regret now.

I can imagine.

But, of course, at the time I didn't have enough money to buy in London, whereas you could buy outside a lot more and I always believed in spreading my risk. We bought all over the country not just locally.

Right and I guess if you bought around here in Docklands 30 years ago you'd probably be fairly comfortable today.

Well yes, if only. You mustn't dwell on the deals you haven't done and some of the best deals are deals you don't do if it goes wrong of course, so you're best not to have done them in the first place.

True.

But you mustn't dwell on the ones that 'oh I wish I'd done this, I wish I'd done that' because at the end of the day you didn't do them and you've done okay anyway, so why worry?

So you see this financial crash coming and then you decide to take a career hiatus where you go into another whole new world again of horse race training.

Well what happened was, after I got sacked if you like from the football club, I thought how am I going to fill my time? I was always an equestrian, I always rode and I met my wife at the Horse of the Year Show - she's a national Dressage rider at quite a high level. So I was always involved with horses, always had horses at home, sadly, because it's a very expensive pursuit as you know. And I've always been very interested in training racehorses. It wasn't about the racing itself on the day, its all about preparing them, a bit like a football club in as much that you're preparing the players for the Saturday game, so it was a bit like that. And I enjoyed it but it's a very, very tough game and what happened was I did it for two years, you do two years to get your licence, so I was qualified to get my licence and then I decided that it wasn't really going forward for me.

I was going to say, because again that's one of the areas where lots of people have started with a large fortune and ended up with a much smaller fortune.

That's how the saying goes yes!

So are you still involved in owning racehorses?

No, I've got some show jumpers with a great friend of mine, Philip Spivey, who is an international show jumper, so I'm a bit of a groupie. I go abroad with him sometimes and it's a good way of relaxing when he's at a big show somewhere, it's great fun.

So having got that out of your system, when was the point at which you thought okay it's time to get back into the property world?

Well, never catch a falling knife, always wait for it to bounce, let someone else take the first risk. We were offered the chance to buy Auction House UK in 2009/2010 and that was a great opportunity for us, I knew the current Directors well, I'd been a client of theirs and they had seven licences at the time around the country as well as running the Norfolk one themselves. They were based in Norfolk, in Norwich, which is a great city, and we decided to invest in that.

And with that I think also came a move back into estate agency?

Yes we actually inherited Fine & Country in Norfolk as part of the deal and I'd vowed never to be an estate agent again, and I'm still not really because although we do own it, I'm not running it everyday. I turn up once a month and buy them all a coffee and do a bit of cheerleading; someone described me as a cheerleader, which I thought was a bit of a cheek; I do a bit more than that but they're all really, really good people we work with and I'm very proud of them all.

John, with 30 years of experience you've moved onto much larger projects like the one on the Ipswich waterfront, tell me about that and how it perhaps differs from some of the smaller things you've done earlier in your life?

At one point we used to buy tower blocks off local authorities in the late 1980s/early 90s and refurbish them and sell them to first time buyers. And then the property recession came and we changed our tactic to doing some listed buildings; we've converted a lot of listed buildings. I've always tended to do things which are slightly more difficult and different to everyone else. That way you make better margins and you've got less competition.

So the one in Ipswich, when I saw the work had stopped in 2008, 150 flats, it was in a shell form, I kept looking at it until 2014 thinking is it time to buy it, is it time to buy it, and I might have jumped in a little bit early but we agreed to buy it in 2014 and completed in 2015. We managed to fund it via the Government Homes England Scheme and we borrowed £20 million to refurbish it, to finish the job and we finished in December 2018.

Money & Me

That's remarkable to have that amount of patience to wait all those years before making your move. I guess that takes a certain kind of character and personality?

Well to be honest with you, normally I'm very impetuous but it doesn't pay to be sometimes. How I look at it is it's like almost paying yourself to be patient, you're making a lot more money by being patient and if I make a lot more money I can definitely be patient!

Right okay. But I think for some people a project like that might seem like a dream to do something on that scale. What would you say is the best way for someone to look at getting involved in the property world today?

Well one of the simplest ways Graham I think is auctions because people always say to me you know John where do I start, how do I get going, how do I do it, can I do it with no money? Well the answer is no, you can't do it without any money, you either need a backer or you need at least 25-30% deposit and if you haven't got that then I know people will tell you you can but it's very, very difficult and I don't want to mislead anyone. So having got a deposit or a backer, I think auctions are a great route and the reason I say that is because the catalogue has got the deals in there already. You can practice without actually buying, you can look at them and go to the auction and see what happens, get involved and I think it's a great way to start, especially if you just want to keep it simple to start with, just do a property up. Buy something that needs a bit of refurbishment, refurbish it, sell it and go again.

And would you propose that people should be doing that refurbishment work themselves to save money?

If they've got a talent for it yes, but if not you're not actually going to be saving any money because the standard needs to be good these days. I mean you wouldn't want me doing it that's for sure; my wife says I can't even screw a door knob on, so you wouldn't want me doing it, you're far better to be out there looking for the next deal and let someone who knows what they're doing do it. But you must be disciplined with them, you want to know exactly what it's going to cost before you start, you want to have an agreement of what you are going to be doing, don't just tell them oh just get on with it, you need a fixed price and get it organised.

You talked earlier on about waiting six years to pounce on this project in Ipswich, one of the things that I've seen in an auction room is people start getting emotional, they get connected to a project, they've done all the work, they want it and they start bidding ridiculous amounts for it.

Yes, well with Auction House UK, (which we built from seven franchises to 42 and I sold my shares last year at which point it was the number one auction house in the UK), what we found was Homes Under the Hammer were a great help to us. Every morning they're on, it increased so many more people getting involved and these people are amateur investors but they need education, and unfortunately some of them just go along thinking you're going to get a cheap bargain and actually you could buy something cheaper down the road on occasions, not always.

You've got to pick what you buy.

And I know you're increasingly involved now in education for people because I see a lot of people who come into the sector not even knowing about some of the major tax changes that have gone on recently for example. Are you seeing this kind of lack of knowledge?

Yes, very much so and it does concern me, it really genuinely concerns me because what I don't want to do is mislead anyone. And sometimes they might look at it and think actually it's not for them, in which case you've done a good job because you've stopped someone getting in all sorts of financial difficulties. Not everyone will make a good investor, not everyone will make a good property developer - there are some fantastic property developers out there, a lot more successful than me, but there's a lot that aren't.

And also I think there's a caveat emptor here, which is be careful who you get your training from because I speak at a lot of these property investment shows and some of these so-called gurus are still peddling strategies that might have worked a decade ago but certainly wouldn't today.

Well this is all a bit new to me because after 40 years as a property developer I'm hard-nosed, and it's interesting but there seems to be an awful lot of people who have been on some courses and then decide that they're experts. With all due respect, they're not experts. I learn every day, every day is a school day, you learn something new every day and that's after 40 years.

So how do you try and structure the training when you get a group of people coming to your events, what are the main things you think you need to focus on?

I start off with the basics, but I don't treat them like children, I expect them to be able to write down themselves any information I've given them that they find interesting and they think will help. I give them examples of how I've done it right and how in the past I've done it wrong and I treat them with respect but also straight forward. If I think something isn't going to work I tell them. If they say to me look John, I want to do this, I might say well don't do it, it's not a good idea. So I give straightforward honest advice. They may not always like what they hear but it's normally right!.

We couldn't talk about the whole property world divorced from the economy, which of course is linked to politics, which brings us to the famous Brexit topic.

Yes.

What are your thoughts on where this is all going to end up and how it might impact the property market?

Well it's very interesting, I'm Chairman of the Ipswich Conservative Association so I have got a bit of a foot in the door at Westminster, and certainly outside London it's not had a massive effect. Certainly, there are plenty of people buying property outside London. Inside London I know it's a bit different, it's like a different world almost and it has had a bigger effect. But then we've also had Stamp Duty, we've had foreign investors not buying anymore for the moment, so it's not just Brexit.

Right.

But outside, you know most people outside London and outside Scotland voted to come out, so actually they are all very positive of course. So it's very, very interesting.

So I guess the corollary of that would be that probably outside of London is the best place to be looking for property deals at the moment?

I think it's the safest place although of course, there's nothing wrong with a bit of turbulence in property as you know Graham, so actually there are opportunities. If there's uncertainty and you are certain of what you're doing and you're certain of what's going to happen, you can make more money out of a difficult market than you can out of a very hot market.

And of course for me, watching this slow motion train wreck unfold in Westminster, one of the things that never seems to get enough attention is the possibility of a snap election and a change of Government. If we're to believe what's being said at party conferences and the like, we're into rent controls, capital controls and all the rest of it, which could massively impact the market.

Well if Labour gets in God help us; there's going to be massive, massive changes. I mean you've got to remember that the Government have brought in a £10 billion Help to Buy Scheme, £10 billion, it's unbelievable. And now for the first time since 1995 first time buyers are the biggest section of the market and that's a remarkable achievement for this Government, bearing in mind they've got Brexit to deal with and everything else as well, it can all change very quickly.

Indeed, I guess the fear is people just think that' oh well they've had a chance and they've messed things up, lets give someone else a go' and suddenly we end up with Jeremy Corbyn.

Well very interesting, of course they haven't messed it up; we've got the lowest employment figures since 1975, so actually the economy is doing amazingly well, especially considering we're in this Brexit situation.

Yes, I guess the area we've got to focus on would be trying to increase productivity, which the stats on that are not so good. But that's more about investment and new plant and machinery or whatever and new technology.

Exactly and people are probably holding back a little bit, but you know at some point this Brexit deal will be done.

Okay, well in closing John, I can't let you go without asking you to give your top two or three nougats to any property investors or potential property investors that are reading this today.

Thanks for putting me on the spot Graham, that's very kind of you! What I would say, I would give you one. And that is especially at auction, why is that property in the auction? That's the question you need to ask yourself every single time, you look at a property that is in an auction, why is it there? Ask the agent or the auctioneer, but don't just take their word for it, go and talk to the next door neighbour because the next door neighbour is more likely to tell you the real reason why it's in the auction.

Okay, lovely. And the final question for you, you've told us about your upbringing and your business environment, what's the advice you would give to your own children and the next generation around the whole money and investing topic?

Get into property; buy something as soon as you can. Make sacrifices to do so.

Fantastic, okay great advice there, John Howard thank you very much for joining us.

It's a pleasure.

Three Key Lessons
From John Howard

1. **Patience is a virtue!** John waited six years watching an abandoned development on the Ipswich waterfront before making his move to buy it. Even then, he thought he might have blinked too soon. Don't be in a rush, there's always another deal around the corner and it may better than the one you're looking at.

2. **Difficult markets can be more profitable.** If you know what you're doing, and you have the right strategy, you can do things differently from the crowd and make serious money. This is an advanced strategy for experienced developers, so don't try this at home...

3. **Why is the property in the auction?** Ask the estate agent and the auctioneer, then verify the situation with the next door neighbour. There's usually a reason why the property has been put into an auction rather than being sold through a conventional estate agent. Knowing the reason will help you determine whether you've found a bargain or a lemon.

Section 5

The Celebrities

John Inverdale

James Max

Aidan Meller

John Inverdale

John Inverdale
Wimbledon Legend

John Inverdale was born in 1957 in Plymouth, Devon, the son of a Royal Navy dental surgeon. He was educated at Clifton College, Bristol and at the University of Southampton, graduating with a history degree in 1979. He gained a post-graduate journalism qualification at University of Wales then spent two years at the *Lincolnshire Echo* before joining BBC Radio Lincolnshire in 1982.

A Sports Stalwart on Radio

John progressed to the BBC's national radio stations in 1985, firstly with Sport on 2 and then on Radio 5's *Sport On 5*. In 1994 he became one of the main regular presenters on the relaunched BBC Radio 5 Live. He presented the drivetime show *John Inverdale Nationwide* until 1997, for which he was named Sony Broadcaster of the Year in 1997. At 5 Live, he hosted the topical show, *Any Sporting Questions*, a variation on Radio 4's *Any Questions*, and similarly toured the UK each week. In 2008 he broadcast for 5 Live from the Olympic Games in China. Along with Sir Steve Redgrave he appeared at Shunyi Rowing Lake for the Olympics in Beijing. Inverdale headed 5 Live's coverage of Wimbledon, the Olympic and Commonwealth Games, football and rugby union World Cups, World Athletics Championships, Ryder Cup, Open Championship, London Marathon and Cheltenham Festival.

He has hosted the station's coverage of BBC Sports Personality of the Year and occasionally guest presented on Radio 2. John left 5 Live in March 2019.

A Sometimes Controversial Television Treasure

From 2000–2014 John Inverdale presented *Today at Wimbledon*, BBC Two's nightly tennis highlights, until the format changed in 2015. This was mainly due to the 2013 Marion Bartoli controversy which led the BBC to drop Inverdale from the show. However, the new version *Wimbledon 2Day* hosted by Clare Balding was ridiculed by the public. Such was the unpopularity of *Wimbledon 2Day*, a Twitter campaign called "bring back John Inverdale" attracted thousands of supporters, with Inverdale claiming that he had "never been so popular." The unpopular highlights show was ditched in 2016 and rebranded with its original title, *Today at Wimbledon*. Inverdale is now a member of the main commentary team.

John became the BBC's main Rugby Union anchor in the 2006 Six Nations Championships and led ITV's Rugby World Cup coverage in 2015. He presents the BBC's World Cup and Olympic Rowing coverage alongside Sir Steve Redgrave. Inverdale has hosted ITV's live French Open coverage from Roland Garros since 2012.

In October 2012, John filmed several episodes of the Channel 4 show *Countdown*.

My guest in this chapter is one of Britain's best known and best loved sports commentators, who has been involved in everything from the Olympics to rowing, from rugby to Countdown, perhaps best known of all of course for Wimbledon tennis. His name is John Inverdale. John welcome to Money & Me.

Lovely to be here, I like your office, I like your view!

It's not bad is it, it's not Broadcasting House that's for sure. So John - you were born in Plymouth, the son of a Royal Navy dentist I think? Tell me a little bit about your upbringing and whether things like money were ever discussed in the family.

I don't think the word ever crossed my mind until I had left university actually. We lived in different places all the time, you know 18 months here, two years there, we lived out in the Far East for a few years, came back to Hampshire then I went to school in Bristol, then to university in Southampton and Cardiff. So you were always dotting around.

I think it's very interesting, when you get to a certain stage in life you do yearn for roots. When somebody says to you 'where's your home' and you haven't really got one, you can't say 'that is where I am from' I do think you're missing out on something but, conversely, I think if you've lived in the same place your whole life you've missed out as well. Because I think if you move endlessly, by the very nature of your life, you have to be a bit more gregarious, you have to make friends otherwise you find yourself being quite lonely. But you get to a certain stage, when people say 'where exactly are you from', I say 'I don't know really', I kind of say London now because I've been here for 30 years, but I wouldn't say this is home, I'm still looking for home!

What would your earliest memories be in terms of when you thought you might want to be in journalism, in commentating - it's not the obvious career choice, where did that come from?

No its not. There was a guy called Alan Gibson, who was one of the very first voices on Test Match Special; I think in 1949, he was a friend of my father's because he'd worked on the Western Morning News down in Plymouth. He came round for dinner one night and he'd just come back from an Ashes

Tour to Australia, which were real tours in those days that went on for months, sometimes it felt like years. He spent the whole of the dinner, three or four hours, talking about how he'd been in Sydney and been in Perth and just been watching cricket and then he filed some reports and then he went to the bar. And I was I think 13 or so and I thought that sounds like quite a good life to me, where can people apply for these jobs? He said he fell into it in the way that people of that generation tended to - it's now a much more clinical operation to get to that stage by doing media studies degrees and all that sort of stuff.

So I made the conscious decision then. I thought right, I've got to be the Editor of the school newspaper and then I went to university and I was Editor of the university newspaper. After that, I graduated at just the wrong time because Margaret Thatcher's first battle in many ways was with the newspaper industry or the print industry.

Yes that's right I remember. I was working for the Daily Telegraph in Fleet Street at the time.

And so I applied for endless jobs on heaven knows how many, literally hundreds of newspapers, literally from Aberdeen to Penzance and the absolute nadir one morning in the summer of 1979, was getting 13 rejections in the post in the same day, which I remember vividly. I remember this cascade of letters through the letterbox and the dog going mad because there were so many letters there and me thinking, on the law of averages, one of these is going to say we quite like the cut of your jib. At least come for an interview, and every single one said thanks but no thanks. And that was a very, very low moment when I thought I was never going to get a job in the industry at all.

And then I did get offered a job by Northcliffe Newspapers as they were then, and I went for an interview in London and they said you know, if we were minded to give you a job would you mind where we sent you? And I thought that was opening me up with the opportunity to specify somewhere and them saying 'no get lost!' So I said, no send me anywhere. And literally the following Monday I got a phone call saying we've got a job for you in Lincoln, would you like it? I said 'absolutely, always wanted to go to Lincoln'. Put the phone down and the first thing I did, absolutely the first thing I did, was I went outside and I got the map out of the car. I thought where the hell is Lincoln? And I ended up spending six incredibly happy years there, so it's funny the way these things turn out.

It is, but also in a sense it may not have felt it at the time, but it seems like some fairly meteoric progress because I think you were still in your 20s when you started working for Radio 2 in sport weren't you?

Yeah I was 28. Having said that, I was quite young then but you'd be geriatric now because everything has moved on and I think if you got onto national radio before you were 30 you were the exception that proved the rule really in those days. Yes I was, I did the early morning stuff, getting up at 4:15 in the morning, but I'd done that on local radio for several years as well. And I think that actually, one of the legacies of doing that for so many years, I think it really impacts on your sleep patterns. If anybody is reading this who has any kind of knowledge of these things, they may say I'm talking complete rubbish, but I do think doing early shifts and getting up at 4 o'clock in the morning for six or seven years is a problem. I've never been a great sleeper ever since. And I just wonder if it's the legacy of that period because the panic, the absolute sheer fear that you're going to sleep through the clock because if you do it's not like other jobs in a sense that somebody can always answer the phone for you. If you're going to be on the radio and you sleep through the clock there's nobody there to do it.

And I had one absolutely awful experience, I can remember the date because you always remember the date when these things happen - it was 22nd November 1986. Now 22nd November is a very significant date in the sporting world because it was on that day in 2003 when we won the Rugby World Cup against Australia in Sydney. But when I think of 22nd November, I always think of 1986; I was doing the breakfast show on local radio and on a Thursday I used to allow myself one lunchtime pint a week, because if you do a breakfast show, and I'm sure anybody from little local radio stations to Chris Evans and all points in between would say the same thing, if you're doing a daily breakfast show you desperately want the Friday programme to be really good because then, over the weekend, you've got two days to say actually I wasn't too bad on Friday as opposed to mulling over the fact that it wasn't very good and you can't wait for Monday to rectify the wrongs of Friday if you like.

So I used to have a routine that on a Thursday I would go to a pub called The Generous Britain, I'd have one pint in there and I'd go to bed, wake up, go rugby training on the Thursday night and then feel replenished, ready to go on the Friday. But on this particular Thursday I had my pint, I went to bed, I woke up, looked at the clock, it said 5:55 and I thought it was 5:55 the following morning and I was on air five minutes later. I was just completely combobulated by fear and panic and oh my God; no mobile phones or anything.

And so I jumped in the car, drove 100 yards down the road, crashed straight into three vehicles that were coming towards me because it was 5:55 in the evening and I thought it was 5:55 the next morning and nobody was on the road and I was half asleep and I just sat at the wheel as all these people were banging on the side of the door, going 'what's wrong with you?' And I just sat there thinking 'what have you done, you idiot?'

I'm sure a lot of people who work around here are on the 6:03 every morning or something, I think in the end that cannot be good for you, it must mess you up in some way or other.

Absolutely. But then you progressed into Radio 5 and a lot of sports coverage and then, very shortly after that, into television. So how did that transition to TV come about, was that just a lucky break?

Yeah it was totally a lucky break. It was a phone call at home – this will make me sound like a really modern man when I wasn't at all at the time – but in 1988/89 BSB, British Satellite Broadcasting and Sky were the first contenders in the cable-satellite war. And a guy who worked for BSB, who'd I'd met at some function or other, he was an ex-BBC person, rang me up and literally I was doing the ironing in the way that you did in those happy single days when someone had to do it. And the phone went and this guy called Nick Hunter was on the phone, he said 'Nick Hunter here, I'd like to talk to you about a presentation opportunity in television'. And I went 'Nick off' and put the phone down because I thought someone was just pretending. And then he rang me back about half an hour later and I said 'are you serious?' and he said 'yeah'. I went for a screen test and a fortnight later myself and Richard Keys were the first two broadcasters on British Satellite Broadcasting.

And then of course however long it was after that, suddenly in that amazing book, I don't know if you ever read it, called 'Dished', if you're talking about financial wizardry and also how it's almost like a game of Russian Roulette. How BSB blinked on the Friday when Sky were going to blink on the Monday and if they hadn't had this board meeting on that Friday afternoon, if they'd said look I'll tell you what, lets sleep on it over the weekend and then we'll reconvene on Monday or Tuesday next week and decide whether we're going to jack it in. And if Sky had met on the Monday, who knows how different broadcasting would have been? So it's a fascinating book and we were right in the middle of it and one moment we were employed and the next moment you were out.

But at least you'd made the break on the television at that point.

Yeah and the great thing about doing it, with all due respect to everybody who was involved in that time and we all knew it when we were doing it, the audiences were beyond negligible, so you could be absolutely hopeless but you were learning on the job.

Yes of course.

And I don't have a single VHS as it would be, of any of those programmes, which I think is probably a good thing, but if I did I'd probably look at them and cringe. But you've got to start somewhere and if you look what Satellite Television has done now, and especially in the context of sport, it has revolutionised our lives.

People talk about the good old days when the only live football match on television was the FA Cup - those weren't the good old days, it was awful. It was terrible the fact that Match of the Day was all you had and that was it every week. I think that the range of choice that we have at the moment now and the way it's covered is just fantastic.

After losing out in the satellite wars, things turned mainstream didn't they John - you became a fixture on our televisions, especially with things like Today at Wimbledon.

Yeah it started in the early-to-mid 1990s and then I was sort of playing Box and Cox with radio and television. And I look back on those days now, 1993 to 2008, and I don't really know how I had time for anything else because I was so busy. And I loved it! The one thing I would always say, and its quite interesting, I've watched a few of your Money & Me programmes and it's quite interesting how people talk about work and what is the definition of work. For me work has just been fun, I think that's the key thing. I don't ever recall, genuinely, waking up in the morning and thinking God I wish I wasn't doing that. And that is a ludicrously fortunate position to be in.

Not even at the time of the controversy after the comments about Marion Bartoli?

Well those were difficult times; when you're the subject of a lot of media furore it's a very strange world to be in the eye of a storm when normally you're on the touchline if you like, looking in on things. But it's a slightly bizarre world being on radio, especially on radio, not so much television because there are too many people involved in television, but radio is quite a singular world. Okay there are producers and there's this, that and the other but fundamentally it's you and a microphone, it's a very intimate world and you can lose yourself. All the rest of the world can be happening around you but in that moment when the red light's on and you're talking about whatever it might be, or you're interviewing somebody or reading this, that and the other, you're just loose in your own little world, a world that you're sharing with your listeners, I think that's the absolute key thing, you know it's our world, it's not my world, its our world and other things just kind of fade away – it's very strange.

The moment you say 'well thanks very much for listening and see you next week' or tomorrow or whatever it might be, suddenly, click, the real world comes and hits you on the head again. But it is a kind of an escape from everything else that's going on whatever everything else might be.

Well there must have been some satisfaction from the fact that eventually they changed the whole format of Today at Wimbledon and there was a huge reaction against it, there was a 'Bring Back John' campaign and lo and behold you did come back.

Yeah well I think there's a Bring Back John campaign a bit like Brexit campaigns - they get listened to or they don't get listened to. In truth I never went away, it's a bit of an urban myth that I suddenly wasn't there. I actually went from presenting straight to commentating so I didn't ever miss a Wimbledon, but that didn't fit the narrative of the agenda that some people had.

But Wimbledon is an amazing event and when you do something for a very long time, and this will be my 34th Wimbledon for the BBC this year, sometimes you do think do you know, wouldn't I like to just go and watch it and just sit and spectate? But it's such a magical event it really, really is and on that very first morning, if anybody knows the geography of that area, you used to drive up from the top of Wimbledon village and laid out in front of you is the All England Club. Honestly on that first Monday in July or whatever it happens to be, I do do that every year and I go, 'there is absolutely nowhere else in the world I'd rather be', it is fantastic.

Yes, it's magical isn't it.

It is.

But I know you also have a love of horse racing, although I believe it hasn't always been your most successful endeavour?

Well you know if this is a money programme here's a money tale that sadly is Wall Street crashing and burning. Yeah I owned a quarter of a horse in 1996 that won a selling race at Leicester on the Monday as I was flying back from the Atlanta Olympics. I got home and – those were the days of answerphones – I listened to the answerphone and the horse had won and it had been bought by Martin Pipe, one of the great national hunt racing trainers of all time. And on the Wednesday I got a phone call from one of the other owners saying Martin Pipe would like to offer me a half share in this horse for £5,000. And actually this horse had won at Leicester and I thought God we'd got rid of this damn thing and we'd probably just about broken even on it, so in horseracing terms, as anybody reading this who has ever owned a leg of a horse will tell you, you're really quids in if you've come out of it without anything in the debit column.

So I ummed and ahhed about it, I looked at it and I just didn't have £5,000 to do it. So rang back and said look I'm really sorry, I'd love to, I'd really, really love to, I'd love to own a horse with Martin Pipe because he was at the peak of his powers at the time as the sort of leader of racehorse trainers. And anyway I didn't do it. That was in August. The following March, this horse called Make a Stand, having won seven races and £1 million in prize money in the intervening period, then won the Champion Hurdle at Cheltenham. I was presenting the Champion Hurdle at Cheltenham and had to congratulate Martin and all those concerned on Make a Stand winning the Champion Hurdle, when all the way through I was thinking 'this was my horse, it was almost my horse'. I've loved horseracing all my life, this was my moment. And just for the lack of that relatively small investment I haven't got anything to show for it!

And it was one of those terrible moments, I mean really awful moments that, as Make a Stand was coming to the last flight of hurdles – and Wimbledon, Cheltenham and probably the Millennium Stadium, the Principality Stadium in Wales, those are my three great citadels of sport – as Make a Stand was coming to the last flight it was that terrible moment, that real kind of Yin and Yang moment about nice you is thinking, 'I'm so happy for Martin and Tony McCoy, who was riding him, I'm so happy for them all that they're going to have one of the great moments in the sun'. And the bad bit of you is going, 'I just hope it falls'. I don't want anybody to get hurt but I just hope it falls because then I might feel a whole lot better. But mercifully I think the good side of me just about held stay, you know.

Fantastic. Well I assume as your fame and your employment level increased your income would increase. So were you able to start putting some kind of investment and savings strategy in place as your career progressed?

I think my family would say to you that I have the business acumen of a pea. But I think in terms of living in London, if you bought a house at the right time, when you probably couldn't afford to, you just got lucky. That ends up being your equity and I'm a great believer that you don't take it with you so what I get I tend to try and spend on whatever it might be. Having odd legs of racehorses; sponsoring my local rugby club, all that kind of stuff. I'm not an investor as such because who knows what's going to happen tomorrow?

So I always think money is related to how you view life generally and I think I'm a great believer in living each day as though it's your last, you know. If you keep putting things away for a rainy day you might never get there.

No that's true enough, but I suppose there's somewhat of a precarious nature to employment in the field you've chosen?

Oh hugely, I mean we're freelancers and at any moment somebody can say 'yeah you were good last year but I think we need a change'. And if you say why, there's often not a very rational argument, its just 'we need a change'. So, as a consequence of that, yes absolutely , you're here today and you could be gone the day after tomorrow.

So there is that. I think you probably just have to have a bit of faith in yourself. You think 'well actually I've done this for so long now that if it all fell down tomorrow I think I'd get something somewhere, I think somebody would employ me wherever it might be'. Maybe I will go back and do the breakfast show on a local radio station and love it because it's great fun, but I'm not sure I'd be very keen on those 4 o'clock starts again you know...

You recently left Radio 5 after 25 years, so you've got some time and some mental space to think. What are the plans? What next for John Inverdale?

I really don't know, its one of those interesting things - I stopped but you know the old cliché about always leave the party while you're having fun? In those long lost days before Uber the number of times I sat on roadsides at 3 o'clock in the morning thinking why the hell didn't you leave at midnight when somebody offered you a lift home? Just ridiculous.

So I think you just feel in your heart you've done it. There's nothing more to be done there. But also I think you're just about young enough to throw yourself into something else, you've still got the energy and the desire and the will and the hunger to do it, which perhaps if you left it another three or four years you wouldn't do. So I've still got bits and bobs of contracts for television work all over the place, but I genuinely don't know what's next. But it's quite interesting that the moment you say something like that, people suddenly ring you up and say, 'hi, do you remember we used to work together 14 years ago', yeah I do, 'we ought to have tea'.

So over the next fortnight I think I've got three lunches and two meets in the pubs at six with people I've known over the last 20 odd years or so to discuss who knows, which is actually quite exciting. It's like in 12 months time what might you be doing, I really don't know but its quite fun to think about it.

My impression is your first love is radio and there's a lot going on in the commercial radio space.

Well I do think one of the most extraordinary things about radio is, not just its longevity for obvious reasons, but its popularity. It is still, in this super techno age where you can get everything on your watch and your glasses and God knows what else, people still love radio, they're loving radio almost more than they've ever loved radio. I think what's really interesting, you can get very deep about these things, but as we become more immersed in ourselves that our whole lives are our tablet, we don't talk to anybody we just talk to ourselves the whole time or we talk to people on tablets or on phones. Actually, someone talking with you and talking in a world that you inhabit on the radio becomes a friend even more than they ever did before. So the relationship that you form with listeners is fantastic and it's someone that you've listened to for 20 years but have never met. When they announce they're leaving that programme some part of you is gone, it's very strange.

It's like a bereavement.

It is - there is no logic to it at all.

I've often said, when somebody I listen to regularly on the radio goes on holiday, I just want to ring them up and say how dare you, you are an integral part of my life. Every Thursday when I go to the gym I listen to you on the way there, it is unacceptable for you to not be there this week, how dare you not do that! And I think that relationship that you form between broadcaster and listener across whatever it might be is very, very important and it's very personal. It's one of those things, if you're one half of it, as I've been lucky enough to be over the last 30 to 40 years, it's not something you want to give up forever.

Okay, well we wait with great interest where life takes you next. John Inverdale thanks very much for joining us.

It's a pleasure.

Three Key Lessons
From John Inverdale

1. **Persistence pays** – look at how hard he had to work to find an opening
    in journalism before accepting an offer on a local paper in Lincoln – and
    promptly having to get the map out to see where it was!

2. **Have liquid funds to seize opportunities** – John was offered the chance
    to part own a race horse for £5,000. That horse went on to win millions in
    prize money for its owners. John is clearly a spender rather than a saver,
    and his lack of ready cash forced him to turn down this opportunity.
    Caveat: We are not suggesting that race horses are a good investment
    strategy!

3. **Don't be afraid of change** – at several times in his career John did not
    know what was going to happen next. At the time of our interview he
    had just walked out on a 25 year career at Radio 5. But he's not worried
    about the future, he's excited about what might be coming next. Whether
    you're staring at redundancy or a failing business, stay positive about the
    new opportunities that life is going to put in front of you.

James Max

James Max
From Property to Media Via The Apprentice

James Max is a journalist and radio presenter specialising in current affairs and business issues. He presents the Early Breakfast Show from 5 am to 6.30 am on Talkradio. Other programmes he's presented include the Early Breakfast on BBC Radio London the Weekend Breakfast Show for London speech radio station LBC 97.3 until August 2013. He was a semi-finalist on the first series of the British version of *The Apprentice* television programme.

He's also an advisor on many property and business projects on areas such as business development, social and digital media. Formerly an Executive Director of BNP Paribas Real Estate, James ran four of their businesse and was on the UK Board. He is also an advisor to Stanhope, the developer who purchased the former BBC Television Centre in West London. He has presented the monthly Estates Gazette podcast, Real Talk and is a Trustee of the Royal Albert Hall.

My guest this week first came to national prominence on the original series of the Apprentice, and since then he's gone on to carve out a successful media career, where he is a presenter on Talk Radio and a columnist in the Financial Times as well as being a property expert and consultant to some of the largest projects in London. His name is James Max. James welcome to Money & Me.

Thank you very much.

Now before we talk about the things that perhaps you've been most well known for, I'd like to just turn the clock back a little bit and talk about what it was like when you were a child growing up and your family environment and whether things like money and investing were ever actually discussed around the dinner table?

I was born at a very early age and the last of four, so I've got three elder brothers and when you have three elder brothers to be honest you're more focused on just keeping hold of your stuff because whatever you have they're going to steal. So you soon learn to keep hold of things.

But what I also learnt when I was growing up is, I suppose, an introduction to different kinds of economics. I used to hear my grandparents talk about the good old days and this and that, and I used to think I don't understand, it's all just lovely, it's kind of where we were. But I was growing up in the 1970s and of course what you realise now is that nobody had any money. And so money wasn't really discussed because we didn't have any. I say we didn't have any, look we lived in a great house and I lived in North West London and I'm sure that my life was very privileged compared to a lot of people, but really we didn't go abroad, we didn't do these things, we went on bucket and spade holidays, all that sort of stuff. We just did what everybody else did and you used to try and book your spot to watch a bit of telly that you wanted to watch, say 'Watch with Mother'. And I'd play outside and go on dog walks and I guess the only thing I was really interested in as a child was Lego. I was obsessed by Lego and then I became obsessed by computer games perhaps in my early teens, because they were just beginning to just go exponential and I think you have to do a transition at some point. There comes a time when you have to leave the Lego behind.

But one of the things I didn't realise about Lego is that it does take you on a building journey. I was always fascinated by building things and the whole construction process, I enjoyed the journey of making things like villages and towns then knocking them all down and starting. This was probably a precursor to 'hello property industry!'

Yes I was going to ask you about that because most of us are clueless about what we're going to do when we're teenagers and yet you seemed to have this quite well thought through strategy, you went to university to study property and straight into the industry, so was Lego responsible for that?

I think Lego was partly responsible but there were other things as well. My grandfather was in the cloth business but he had a side interest, he really liked property, he thought property was great. So I guess there was quite a lot of discussion about property kicking about the house. My dad was a property lawyer, so having seen my eldest brother go into the law, I just thought 'you know what, no thanks', and I studied this new subject called urban geography when I was at school. It wasn't about oxbow lakes and mountains and tectonic plates and stuff, which I found rather tedious, it was about changing environments, the human environment, the things that are required and it kind of tied in with economics. And I really found economics and geography fascinating and I really enjoyed it and so that's what I did for my A-Levels.

And I remember coming down to where we are now pretty much (*the Isle of Dogs in London's Docklands – GR*), and standing on the vacant site and being told this is going to be the most amazing development site in Europe, this is going to be a financial capita. They were just beginning to clear the site and you thought 'hang on a second, this is just a load of old docks, what are you talking about, it's a ridiculous idea!'

And here we are.

And here we are. But then I guess I'd also been introduced to massive schemes, and I remember being taken as a small child to Brent Cross when it had just opened. I must have been 6 or 7, and I thought 'oh this is amazing', an indoor shopping centre, it had this amazing fountain and as a small child you loved these things, it was kind of like the American model.

The papers, when you go back and have a look at how it was received when it opened, 'white elephant', 'disaster', no one's going to shop like this, who wants to go and hang out in a shopping centre, are they all dull, blah, blah, blah and of course history tells you that it was a very smart move and within a year or two it was of course booming. It was the West End in North West London.

So I suppose I was always interested in things like that and how the built environment can change the place in which we live. And if you live in London, which is arguably the most diverse and exciting and vibrant city in the world, it reinvents itself in the most staggering and almost brutal way. You see these incarnations, something dies, people lose their jobs, it becomes really quite arid for a period of time. You go further east and you see where Ford used to be and you think this is where the motor industry was born and it died here and then you see what's happening now in terms of its redevelopment even further east than we are here. Here we are at the centre of the docks, this is what made Britain wealthy in the first place, it's making Britain wealthy again.

People reinvent themselves and to be honest, its not the most convenient spot in the world to build, its not the most convenient spot to be located, we're an island, all these challenges and yet it's the brains which are available, people want to do these things, they want to use London as this trading post, almost against all odds. There are plenty of other places which are far more convenient and probably have far cheaper access to all sorts of infrastructure which is there already. No, no, we're going to build it so we'll build the tunnels under the Thames, we'll build the tube lines, we'll build these big buildings, we'll empty and drain the docks, we'll clear the space, we'll redevelop. All sorts of things which were just bonkers but its something which inspires me, I just find it fascinating.

Clearly. And so you go to university, you study land management and property and so on and then you come out and you're straight into some pretty high-powered jobs, a place like DTZ and Morgan Stanley and I think you became a Chartered Surveyor...

I did.

You were very much into some very juicy property projects. So actually you started living the dream almost as soon as you graduated.

Yeah so when I left university I wasn't quite sure which bit of the industry I wanted to be in but I started doing city valuations and various other things that you have to do for your formal training. And I think it was there that I got exposure to doing investment deals and this particular job came up working with this chap and he was looking to bring German capital into the UK. It was a bit new and everybody thought this was a bit, how shall I say, off beat. But I think when I joined the team, they'd just done the first big deal and they'd been pushing for this for three years.

And I was very lucky, I was lucky that I arrived in a team that was really busy, that had really found this niche that nobody else was doing. And also I prefer buying property to selling it, selling it anybody can do, it's like here it is, here's the price, sell. Buying property is difficult, buying property away from the market process is even more difficult, working out what you should pay for it, how do you make it make money, how do you finance it, how do you structure it, how do you get the capital in? How do you make sure that people understand that you are someone who is credible and then how do you make it work from a tax perspective once you've bought it so it performs and that income performs?

All of those questions I found fascinating and for six and a half or seven years I worked with this team, we built the team and I worked with this Director, a chap called John Rigg, who had an enormous amount of experience and was one of the most brilliant people I've ever worked with. And we put this team together, it was great fun, friends for life kind of thing, and I guess when it came to it, I suppose I felt that I'd gone as far as I could with it.

And Morgan Stanley had knocked on my door and the Americans were coming and some people said 'oh the Americans, they've been coming for the last 20 years, you know they're never going to make it, they're never going to come over'. But the thing is that they were here and they'd started to do this private equity fund acquisition stuff, they'd started to do really mega deals, but at a corporate level where you needed to understand real estate, they wanted somebody who understood real estate.

So I was the first English guy to join the team and it was a team of about eight of us. Three and a half years later, when I left, there were 90 of us! I mean it was mega, so it was great fun.

Pioneering days, so you worked on some really big projects as Morgan Stanley came over to the UK?

Yes – at DTZ or Cushman & Wakefield as they're now called, I think we did £6 billion worth of acquisitions and development funding and all sorts of things, so a lot of big deals. And then Morgan Stanley, the first thing I worked on was the IPO as in taking public of Canary Wharf Group. The second thing I worked on was the securitisation of Broadgate, which was £1.6 billion of debt secured against this massive great big scheme above Liverpool Street Station. I and the team sold a whole load of assets all across Italy for ENI, which is an oil company who had all this real estate everywhere; that was bonkers.

So what were the main learnings you took from those two roles, because you come straight out of university into these great opportunities, at that early stage of your career you must have felt that you were really going places in the real estate business?

Yeah totally; I think I learned that if you work hard you should be able to make it. I think I learnt sometimes from being the right side of the coin and sometimes from being the wrong side of it that not everything goes to plan. I think that you learn about relationships as well with people, both within your team that its really important to have respect and trust for the people that you work with and as soon as that goes or if that goes, then you perhaps shouldn't be there.

I think you learn also about the importance of relationships outside of business. The people that I've met along the way I tend to remain in touch with. I remember leaving DTZ at the time and they said 'oh well you know, bye bye, we'll never see you again kind of thing'. And in fact I've stayed in touch with people because I think people assume that you're just going to go off and never think of them again, but when you've worked with people and you've really enjoyed it or you've got a lot of time for them and a lot of respect for them, you want to stay in touch with people.

I think it's a key lesson isn't it that business is all about relationships and why shouldn't those relationships endure when you're no longer working alongside people?

There is a sort of sneery comment, 'its not what you know, its who you know' and when people start to sneer at the 'who you know', in fact it's very difficult to get to know the right people and that is sometimes undervalued in terms of what that can do. And there are still people today that I can call and have conversations with if I need to or if I want to and it saves a lot of time.

Okay, we've covered your first career, I now want to talk about when the call came for a certain programme and how that opened up a new career for you. So James, tell me about this moment in your life when you think you're already flying high doing all these big real estate projects and then somebody, presumably from the BBC, rings up and says 'we're doing this new programme called The Apprentice, would you like to be on it?' What actually happened?

Not that! After Morgan Stanley, I'd gone to work for private equity firm, the first year was great, the second year, hmm, third year, pretty horrendous. And it was pretty horrendous because when your mentor leaves either you should take your mentor's job or you should probably go too. In private equity you are a partner within a business and as a partner within a business you want to do everything possible to be what's called a good leaver. And I wanted to be a good leaver because the money that I had tied up was quite significant, so we're talking probably seven figures, and so you don't want to lose that. So is it worth going off and doing something utterly bonkers to ensure that you are a good leaver as opposed to doing something that might risk it?

So for example, I couldn't go and work for another investment bank, an investment fund, a private equity fund for a period of about three years because you have to wait for everything to vest and then you have to wait for everything to go and I think my contract said 18 months or something like that.

So I thought right, well here's something and a friend of mine sent me a link and they said look they're casting for this new TV show, why don't you have a look at it and I thought, well I can apply and see what happens. So I applied and then I forgot about it. And then they got in touch and then I sent something else and then they got in touch again and then I went for some interviews and then on the day that everything vested to me in terms of all my positions in this real estate fund, I got the call to say we'd like to invite you to be one of the 16 or whatever it was! I was on holiday at the time and I remember ringing up the boss and saying 'right okay, well that's me done, so I'll be handing in my notice now'. And there was all this kafuffle and all this, like you can't go dah, dah, we're about to launch a fundraiser. I said I didn't like the offer, I told you I didn't like the offer before I went on holiday and this isn't for me and thanks.

And in fact there were a couple of people there that I just didn't want to work with and I never really want to see them again. The people I did enjoy working with, they'd all left. So I think that was why I made the comment before about at the time that you are not happy with the people you're working with, you've got to trust them, you've got to like them, and I really liked the guy who had hired me and I really trusted him, he was great to work with and we're still friends and I have a huge amount of respect for what he's gone on to do; the other people not so much.

So you go on the programme and I know these days people clearly go on it to get their 15 minutes of fame, but in those early series there were some pretty serious candidates - what was the real experience like as opposed to the sort of heavily edited version that the public get to see?

It was amazing, I've never experienced anything like it before or since and I probably never will. I just went in with a very open mind. You have to remember this was the first series, nobody knew what reality TV was and nobody went on to become famous. I certainly didn't, and I still don't consider myself as being particularly fame hungry, I'm not interested in being famous. I'm interested in being well known for what I do, but I think that's a very specific thing. So I went on because I wanted to do something completely different and it was as you saw it mostly. They did a couple of things in the edit which I thought were unnecessary and wouldn't be allowed today, because I think they changed the story and I thought the story was compelling enough.

What I also learnt was what people see on screen, what they see on telly, what they see sat on their sofas, that's what happened; so if something else happened behind the scenes that didn't happen if it didn't happen on screen.

So I guess I learnt a few harsh lessons but mostly good experiences from it and it was great fun, I enjoyed it, people like to talk about it, it was fun.

I think the supreme irony is of course now Lord Sugar is so heavily into commercial property; he made a big mistake not hiring you as his Apprentice.

Well that's what Claude Littner says and to be honest, I was genuinely interested in the prospect of working with him but he said 'well why would anybody come and work for me for less money than they were on before', and I said because I dare say you're the sort of person that if I made you a lot more money you might give me some more. I'm really not fussed about, I've never been fussed about the base salary, I'm fussed about what the total compensation package is, and if you've got a deal or if we're doing something interesting then you can share out the rewards.

I was quite relaxed about it and I thought it would be interesting to work with somebody like Alan Sugar. I think I learnt a sort of television lesson – the person who *should* win doesn't necessarily. We've seen it with all the talent shows, other people go off and do interesting things, to be honest, if you get to the last three, four or five you can go off and do something with it if you want to.

Well you certainly did, you built this profile in the media, including doing a long stint at LBC.

I did.

Now you're at Talk Radio doing a business-based show. One of the challenges I always come across is trying to make financial and business things interesting - you're doing this for a mass audience, so how do you make it compelling?

Whatever you do business is right in the heart and centre of what we do. So I know that some people say business is boring, and that's because a lot of the mainstream media coverage of business is boring. Business is not about indices and markets going up and down; that is showing the shape of a curve and sentiment, that's the only thing I take from it. So for example, we'll do a business news roundup and I will mention what the markets are doing, more because I'm interested in where we are psychologically, because business is psychological, half of it is about how you feel and if you are feeling good about something and confident you will probably make investment. If you are feeling bad and conservative about it then you won't.

And so, for example, the B word that everybody likes to talk about, its not that there is a problem either one way or another, I know that remainers and Brexiteers love to talk about the benefits of whichever side, if you wanted to remain then you don't realise that we were a pebble in the European shoe and they hate us, and if you wanted to leave then you don't realise that there were some benefits of being part of the club, you know, it switches both ways.

We're in such a cloud that everybody's getting het up about it and every major decision that's happening - a car company decides that they're not going to be manufacturing somewhere and it's to do with the B word. No, its to do with the fact that we've shut our eyes for the last 24 months, that technology is moving at such a fast pace. The diesel engine has been consigned to the history books because it is a pariah, the petrol engine will have to go within the next ten years. So that means whole new technology, here we are in the docks, back to that again, it's reinvention. So are we going to be able to reinvent and therefore how does it affect you, how does it affect me, what have we got to do to be re-taught, to re-skill, what do we need to know?

So the way I make it interesting is saying look, everything is a business from Ant & Dec on ITV, that's a business, why is it a business, because they're their biggest revenue earner. So when one of them went into rehab and we had to talk about that, that's like one of your real estate assets losing their best tenant for a period of time. How do you deal with it, what does that do to the TV model? Years ago we thought ITV was this massive great big player and it couldn't possibly get any bigger, how dare Virgin come and try and take them over!

Meanwhile now we wonder whether they're going to survive because Netflix and Amazon Prime are huge, Disney, huge, Comcast, huge, global players. We have been left behind, we got stuck for example with the BBC who are an amazing institution that I worked for for a little while, but we didn't reform them in this amazing changing landscape.

The reason why I think you can make business so exciting, where we are today is not going to be where we are even in five years time, the things which are going to change: AI, the impact of technology, the impact of the way that we work. It's not that we won't have to work, it's just that what we do and what is valued is so different.

Years ago people who were on the land growing stuff were really valued. We've stuffed them, now you can get all the money for just being able to take it from A to B, how can that be? So I think it's about making it relevant to you and me and then telling some fun stories and throwing in a sausage here and there.

And finally, a lot of people say to me, 'oh if only I had money all my problems would be over'. And I say no, no, no you just get a different set of problems! And you've really taken this to heart with your FT column called Rich People's Problems. Where did the germ of the idea for that come from and what kind of response have you had to it?

I went for lunch with my now Editor, Claer Barrett, who I've known for a very long period of time. And she used to come onto my show as a guest and I first knew her I think when she was on a property mag years ago. We'd always been in touch, I thought she was great fun and we decided we'd go out for lunch. And I always think that the best meetings are the ones where you don't have an agenda and you don't want anything. And we didn't want anything we were just going to have a laugh and a catch up.

One thing led to another and we ended up hooting with laughter about various things and she said 'God you're bonkers', which is probably right, but then also I said I am sick and tired of everything being about austerity and disaster and crashing markets and all this.

The property market isn't crashing, we are not in a state of crisis, in fact economic growth is great, it's just that we're not allowed to talk about people who are doing well anymore and there's nothing for them. So why don't we take a slightly light-hearted look, tongue in cheek, about the sorts of things that if for example, you're not on the breadline, you will have various different problems and by rich people's problems it can actually apply to anybody. And the whole thesis behind it was 'what is rich?' Rich is somebody who's got more money than you because if I say to you Graham are you rich, are you rich?

Oh absolutely.

Are you?

It's all relative isn't it, I certainly don't feel rich.

No, you see people say to me, are you rich and I would say 'no', because I've got to pay for this, that and the other, and the insurance bill and dah, dah, dah, dah. And then people look at me and they go yeah but... and that's because they're perhaps looking at something else that I may have like a car or something. And then you realise that in fact in relative terms I'm doing okay, so therefore what advice can I impart from the fact that I do have a whole range of problems and suddenly you start talking to people and guess what, you've got problems too!

I remember interviewing a really attractive film star and I said to her look, you are one of the most incredibly attractive people that I have ever met. I'm assuming that you don't wake up in the morning and worry about your looks and they said, 'no I look in the morning and think that looks pretty good'. So I said right fine, because lots of people do worry about how they look, so what do you wake up in the morning and worry about? And then suddenly all these different problems came out and you thought, hang on a second, one of the richest, most successful film stars in the whole world and they've got all these problems? Everybody has problems and as you said, they're different from yours.

So the FT column is all about how we can do that in a slightly humorous way. A lot of people take umbrage to it, the online banter is far better than anything I could write and it's really taken off and it's a hoot. So hopefully people are now seeing it for what it is. You know there's normally a serious message in there somewhere, but it is hopefully a bit of light relief on a Saturday once a month, as people are chewing through their Cornflakes or whatever, thinking you know, the world's not that bad!

Okay, so I'm glad that you're helping to express rich people's problems in the FT every month James. That's all we've got time for so thanks very much for joining us.

Three Key Lessons
From James Max

1. **Follow your dreams** – from his childhood Lego days James wanted to be in the construction industry and went on to achieve great success in multiple senior roles.

2. **Build and maintain a network of contacts** – there's a lot of truth in the cliché that 'it ain't what you know it's who you know'. Relationships are important so work on developing them and don't let them evaporate just because you change roles. Make the effort to stay in touch because you never know when that relationship could come in handy for either of you.

3. **Don't be afraid to re-invent yourself** – just like Docklands has transitioned from run down warehouses to Manhattan on Thames, your career or business can thrive on reincarnation. James has used his appearance on the Apprentice to build a media career alongside his property career. What other talents do you have and how could they be developed to generate new income streams?

Aidan Meller

Aidan Meller

Fine Art Expert and Creator of Ai-Da the Robotic Artist

Aidan Meller is a specialist in modern and contemporary art and, until 2019, ran galleries in Oxford and London. With 20 years' experience in the art business, he works closely with private collectors and is often consulted by those who wish to begin, or further develop their collections. He has helped investors to acquire original works by the likes of Picasso, Matisse, Chagall, John Constable, Turner and Millais.

An author on the subject of the art market and western art history, Aidan has been consulted by the media as an expert in his field, with recent appearances on the BBC and Sky News regarding affairs such as the exhumation of Salvador Dali. The *Aidan Meller Art Prize* has received media attention as a valuable resource for the development of the arts.

Aidan's art discoveries include a collection of Pre-Raphaelite cartoons for stained glass from Heaton Butler and Bayne and Powell & Sons. Celebrated as a major Pre-Raphaelite find, the collection was authenticated by inhouse and external experts.

In May 2019 Aidan's career took a whole new turn with the launch of Ai-Da, the world's first robotic artist controlled by Artificial Intelligence. Since then he has been at the centre of a media storm, appearing in over 900 TV, radio and media outlets. Ai-Da sold out her first exhibition at Oxford University in July 2019 with over £1.6 million of works sold ahead of the event. At the time of writing Aidan is preparing for her second exhibition, expected to be in London in December 2019. Further exhibitions including New York and Shanghai are planned for 2020.

Aidan is living proof that opportunity is always around the corner if you keep your antennae well tuned!

Learn more at aidanmeller.com

My guest in this chapter is one of the country's leading experts on fine art investments. He has run his own gallery in Oxford for 20 years and he has developed a unique system that helps anyone learn how to become an art investor. His name is Aiden Meller. Aiden welcome to Money & Me.

Thank you very much.

Now obviously we'll get onto the subject that's become your life's passion in a moment, but I want to take you back a bit first and put you on the analyst's couch because experts say that our views on money and finance and investing are actually formed at a very early age. So tell me a little bit about the sort of family environment you grew up in and whether the M word was ever actually mentioned?

The M word was used. My father ran a building company and my mother was a teacher and he set up that business as a builder because he was made redundant. So as regards the issue of money, I do remember when I was a small child him trying to set that up and get that all sorted. It was a bit of a stress actually but as the business built he was able then to relax a little bit more. But to see him strive to do that was obviously very valuable for when I set my own business up.

What kind of values did your parents drill into you about money and its importance?

Without a doubt a Protestant work ethic. They really did feel that you earn what you work for and I guess, when I look back, they were very strict on all of that. They were quite disciplined and they did work all hours God sends, especially in those early days. And so yeah, that has been passed down to me as that is what you do.

And did you feel in any way kind of neglected or deprived because of their focus on working so hard to build the business?

No, I guess maybe in hindsight but we're in a different world today than I was when I was a child. My dad did work a lot of the evenings as well and, when I look back at things, would probably have loved to have had that time with him. But who am I to comment when it was harder times then, you know we

213

didn't have the prosperity that we enjoy now, so I guess it's fair enough. I can see what he was trying to do and my respect was there.

And I guess what happened was that his business became successful enough that he was able to send you to a posh school and that I think was when you first started developing an interest in art?

Yes without a doubt. There was a teacher called Geoff Bailey, he was inspirational to me, he was critical in my whole approach to art because he had such a… he spoke about artists as if he knew them. And we'd talk about Picasso, Matisse, Chagall and yet he was well versed enough in those artists to be able to talk about them on quite a personal level, and that made me fall in love with art.

Okay, and then that developed I think even to university; you went on to read art history?

Yes, absolutely, I did a degree in art and university of course was a fantastic thing. I really did feel like I was a caterpillar becoming a butterfly; to have that time away and to be independent when you're in your early 20s, wonderful.

But then I think there was a calling to teaching and an international career that took you to India?

In actual fact, when I left university I really did want to see the world. One thing my mother used to speak of a lot was her excitement of finding out about different cultures. So when I left university I went to India and wow, what a contrast that was! And you've got to remember, in those days there were no mobile phones, there was no connectivity, so when I went to the South of India I was there on my own. I did call home at £1.30 a minute or whatever it was in those days. So yeah, I went to another planet actually rather than another country because it was just so different to what I expected.

So what was the impact on your interest in art because, when you go to India, it has a very different artistic and cultural history?

Well it made me realise, which is similar to the art world, there are different worlds, there are different worlds of art as well, and so to just have an appreciation of that and trying to get into the culture of that, it was really just an exciting time of my life.

But then I think you had some health challenges out there?

Yeah, the only thing is I threw myself probably too much into it, I ate food from the street and I actually became very ill, so badly ill in fact that I had to come home. It was all a bit traumatic and unpleasant. I was rushed into

Leicester Royal Infirmary, the Tropical Diseases Unit and they put this plastic lining in my stomach to stop me vomiting. I had three months then to try and recover and think 'what on earth was that all about?'

So that down time caused a bit of soul searching about what you were going to do next?

I was very low, I really did think I was going to see the world and I was going to have this incredible thing and they were going to have the benefit of my company by being out there. It wasn't that at all, the impact of them on me was incredible and I've got to say, I was humbled beyond belief. In fact, when I got home it was a pretty low period because I didn't then know what to do. My time out there as a teacher was cut short and then I was suddenly back in England, where do I go now?

And that was quite an upsetting period and I was pretty depressed.

And I think it was a question from your father that really ultimately triggered your career change?

He absolutely kicked me into touch.

Really, how?

He did kick me into touch because basically, every time he saw me, I was very negative. And so he understood that for a bit but when I was continuing to be negative he said, 'look I'm fed up of you telling me what you can't do. I know you feel you failed out there, tell me what you can do!' And I thought well, what can I do? Of course I was so negative at that point, thinking I can't do anything, but actually that was not true. So I got a teaching job here and I started to paint, I started to paint my own pictures and actually that is something I could do. And as a result of that I was able to then start putting a whole load of works together and I was even brave enough to go to the local bank and set up a business account and display some of the artwork in the foyer there. It was incredible; in those days you just met your bank manager, and he said yes, come and display them. I did, in the foyer, in the bank, that place you don't buy art from and to my absolute astonishment every one sold! I mean it completely blew me away.

Wow!

And my dad was right, I could do something. So with that little bit of confidence, that tiny millimetre of confidence I was able to then say, okay I'm going to take my wares to other places. I'm going to go to National Trust houses, I was going to do Olympia or the NEC and start showing my work there, which I did.

So in a sense you could say that taking up painting and being an artist lifted you out of depression?

Without a doubt.

Absolutely that tiny little boost of confidence in me when I was feeling so low, absolutely.

And as a result of that, crazy as it sounds; I then had another tiny little misfortune in that I had a very serious car crash. I can still feel the lumps and bumps now from the damage that I had from hitting another car head on. They were from Germany and were driving on the wrong side of the road and we were both going 70, it was pretty bad.

Ooh.

But as a result of that I got a big payout because obviously it was very clear cut who was at fault, and with that money I did something – at the time again these tiny little steps you take – I bought a printing press, so I was able to make editioned copies from my original works. I did that and they sold very well and, as a result of that, then other artists were saying, 'well, could you do that for us?'

So before I knew where I was I had a little publishing company and we eventually employed a friend on a part time basis. I was more terrified for their job than me keeping my teaching job. And as a result of that we got into 500 shops in this country and it started to really broaden.

Anyway, to cut a long story short, I eventually got to 18 staff at that particular business and we then started to sell to America, to Australia, to South Africa and these were prints, cards, posters, the whole thing started to mushroom; an incredibly exciting period.

So that was as a result of, in a sense, your own career as an artist being ironically brought to a stop by the car crash, you then became a purveyor or art including copies of your own work right across the country.

Yes ironically that's right.

And in actual fact it was because I soon realised that we had rockets and snails, as I called them, some works just sold enormous numbers, like we sold to Walmart I think 200,000 cards of this particular image, incredible numbers, and other works we sold maybe three copies of. And so I thought this is not right, what I need is some way of being able to test what these images are doing for people. So as a result of that I did another brave step, again I didn't think of it, in your 20s there's no brave steps you're just so headstrong you just do it, but I set up a gallery and it was that gallery that changed everything.

So Aidan, tell me about your 20 years as a gallery owner and how that's developed.

Honestly you couldn't design this could you? It's so organic in the way that it grew. Basically I wanted a gallery to be able to try out some of these images that we were doing for the publishing company. As part of that we then started to get a whole load of original works in, people got very excited by that and then I had a completely lucky break, and I've got to say this was a lucky break. I saw an opportunity to have some time at Sotheby's Institute, so I went along and that completely blew my mind. They had such a great understanding and bird's eye view of the entire art world. I was with incredibly exciting people and the speakers that they had were from all over the industry, I was hooked and I wanted to then specialise. So, as a gallery, we then started to specialise and I chose modernism. I wanted the big names, the Picasso, Matisse, Chagall, really amazing interesting artists.

So I actually had two very separate businesses, although they were initially together, I then sold the publishing business and focused on the art.

I think what makes it fascinating to me is that you've not just got this interest in and passion about the art history, but you've also become an expert in how the art market works, so you can really help people - in fact you've developed this unique system for how to invest successfully in art. How has that all come about?

I started to realise that there was a huge amount of effort and focus by galleries and the art world on the culture of art - not on the figures of art. So I made it my business to understand some of the figures, I wanted to understand what was trending, I wanted to understand where the biggest money was, I wanted to understand why certain artists were able to very quickly gain certain prices and other artists didn't do that. And it was that realisation, the whole investment side and my understanding and growing maturity in that, that I thought is really compelling.

So does that mean that art has been your default investment of choice in your own portfolio?

I can't see any other industry touching what art can do investment wise; I am utterly sold on that. And because I know the 'underbelly' now, I know how to present it to market in respect of understanding its provenance and what people are looking for, making sure that they're secure, that it is the real, authentic work that we're saying it is and how to prove that. So the whole infrastructure to investment is very important. And as I say, I've created a whole system now to understand that so that people can be really safe in their purchases.

So have you ever ventured into any other areas of investment like property or the stock market?

I have, I've done a little bit of property. My goal is to buy a house a year, which I've kept to. I do enjoy property, it's not nearly as exciting as art but I do it as a way of preparing for my retirement. Eventually I'm not going to do art and in my retirement I would probably want things to be slightly less crazy than they are at the moment. So that's why I've done that.

So what would you say has been your best investment over the years?

I guess really getting expert in a particular area and being able to compare prices. It's simple economics, really understanding what is under value, what is currently exciting in the market and putting the whole thing together so it then becomes very compelling and solid.

What about any investment errors, any mistakes, any cock-ups, what's the worst investment you've ever made?

Worst investment, I guess was actually in property, not art. I bought a property that I thought I could convert into a six bedroom house from a three bedroom house. Of course the planning was a problem, they wouldn't allow me to do what I wanted and in actual fact we sold it. So yeah, you've got to know what you're doing, it's like all things. That is why I've produced this art investment system, because then people have a whole checklist so that they can move forward with confidence.

Now you've got a growing family of your own, what are you teaching your children about money and finance?

Without a doubt, don't just come up with ideas and go for them! I think a lot of entrepreneurs think that's what they should do. I think the real key difference to what I would tell my children now is - work out a problem that people have and really analyse that problem and then get a solution to that problem. So do it from the customer's perspective, don't do it from your own idea. Everybody has ideas, they're worth ten a penny to be fair, so I would say to any entrepreneurs don't just wake up and think you're going to be the next Google just because you've got a great idea, there's lots of ideas, find a problem and fix it.

Okay and what about more basic things like budgeting and saving, do you try and get them to look after their pocket money a little bit?

Absolutely and also to think actually, is this really what you want? There's so much hype and excitement around things you know, the latest fad, do you want to join it, do you want to go and spend a few hundred pounds on that toy when in fact you know that in a couple of months you're not going to be playing with it. They're still very little so you've got to do it in a suitable manner for them.

Absolutely. Now, you deal with a lot of artists and you deal with a lot of art investors, what are some of the biggest financial mistakes that you see other people making?

I guess just going on emotion and believing the galleries who are trying to sell stuff. I am shocked by how many galleries say 'such and such is a great investment' and I'm thinking on what grounds do they claim that because I can't see that being the case at all. So people don't know what they're doing and so they go and believe the gallery, then they go and try and sell it and get barely anything compared to what they originally paid for it. Then they come to us and say what happened, and I say well it was obvious right from the beginning that that wasn't going to be a good investment because the type of work that you've got doesn't appreciate. But they didn't realise that, they just believed the gallery.

So what I would say is get some more security in respect of a tick list, as I say I've got a tick list that says yeah, this is more likely to be much more successful.

If you look at things like the Knight Frank Wealth Report, you can see that art has been one of the best investments over the last 20 or 30 years, but I guess what you're saying is only if you know what you're doing?

Yes, and I think art is very transportable, it's tangible, it doesn't go into the mass markets like stock markets, which can go up and down and it's all about the feeling. Individual pieces can be very compelling, you get top artists, a top name and they don't have to be expensive, you can buy a Picasso for under £100,000, you can buy a Matisse for £20,000, it is still possible. So with small amounts of money you can be very, very successful even with top names.

As Michael Caine might say – not a lot of people know that!

So, as we come to the end of our time together Aidan, what's left on your financial bucket list of things you'd still like to do?

I still love travelling, I've done a lot of travelling in my life and I absolutely love finding out how other people live. People are fascinating and there's many worlds out there. I know we're getting a globalised world and we think it's all homogenising, which is true, but I'd still like to go and do more travel and therefore find out what other investments are out there. There's some incredible cultural art out there - in fact I've just come back from Russia and we bought some unique artworks out there. Yeah, very compelling.

What's been the best piece of art that you've discovered during your 20 years in the business?

There's one that absolutely outshines all the others. I had had a phone call to say 'you sell Pre-Raphaelite works; we have some Pre-Raphaelite works - come and have a look'. So I went along and I could not believe it, there were seven cardboard boxes full of Pre-Raphaelite School works, I was blown away. I buy maybe one or two a year and that's about it, so to have all of these works together was incredible. Obviously I was worried about where they came from – turns out they were bankrupt stock from Powell & Son, which was the largest architects at the time, and they did stained glass window drawings, incredible!

So we came to a price at which everybody was happy. Then I came away and it was at home that, when I did some research, I realised that these were stained glass window drawings for Westminster Abbey, for St Paul's Cathedral and landmark buildings like that. It was knock-out, it couldn't get better!

Wow! So that's the good end of the spectrum. Have there been any others that have got away from you?

Yes I'm afraid so when I look back. About 15 years ago I was offered eight Andy Warhol originals and they were screen prints but priced at between £4,000 and £8,000 each. The cheapest they would be now would be about £200,000 each and the most expensive would be over a million pounds. If I did nothing else but buy those eight Andy Warhol's I'd be a multimillionaire just from that one purchase alone…

Wow. Okay, so if I push you against the wall and put a gun to your head and said 'what's the one piece of investment advice you would give to the people watching us today', what would that be?

Get knowledgeable, be educated – education, education, education because it's from that that I've been able to do what I've done today.

So it's very much 'invest in yourself'?

Yes without a doubt.

Absolutely no hesitation.

Okay brilliant. Aiden Meller, thanks very much for joining us.

Thank you.

Three Key Lessons
From Aidan Meller

1. Focus on what you can do – in Aidan's case it took a question from his father to shake him out of depression by ignoring his past failings and focusing on developing his art skills

2. Invest in your education – only by learning can you acquire the skills to be successful in your chosen career, business or investing activity. As Jim Rohn said 'formal education will make you a living, self education will make you a fortune'.

3. Plan your business from the customer's perspective. Too many entrepreneurs have a good idea then throw time and money at implementing it only to find no one wants to buy it! Far better to find a problem the customer has and help them solve it – like how to invest in art safely and profitably!

51 Key Lessons

1. **Invest in your education** – this can include working a job to get the knowledge you need to launch a business. The more you learn, the more successful you will be in your chosen field.

2. **Personal branding** – Justin's red bow tie, pocket square and braces are as much a part of his success as the words he says in his media appearances. You need to stand out from the crowd more than ever, so pay attention to creating your own brand and be consistent with it as you grow your following

3. **Think of your extended family as a company** and form a Family Office to run everyone's financial affairs. If you can overcome unwillingness to share information, the benefits of scale can be significant. This is especially true for today's complex family structures with multiple generations, multiple marriages with children from each and with the biggest wealth transfer in human history about to go down.

4. **The ability to convey your ideas in writing is a valuable one** – Tim has used his writing in Money Week to enhance his status as a fund manager and his experience as a fund manager to inform his writing. While he has not developed as high a media profile as Justin Urquhart Stewart, he combined writing in the specialist press and speaking at financial events to build his profile and his client base.

5. **In these uncertain times focus on avoiding losses** – this is especially true for those who have already accumulated significant wealth, but applies equally during the wealth building phase. Make sure you spread your risk across different asset classes and watch out for bond prices falling if interest rates rise and watch out for tracker funds that will follow the market down without any proactive corrective action.

6. **Look for great companies available at a price below market value** – the essence of value investing. Be prepared to look anywhere in the world to find them, for example Asia. Be ready to buy more if the price falls rather than copying the crowd who run away when high quality stocks and shares are available at bargain basement prices!

7. **Your client can become your employer** – Lord Fink's big break came after he had done some work for Man Group as a client and they liked what they saw. Whether you are an employee or a service provider, keep your antennae tuned for an opportunity to further your career (provided you do not breach any No Poaching agreements!)

8. **Set up a Family Investment Company** to involve the next generation in managing the wealth you have created. This can also be a highly tax efficient means of passing wealth between the generations if it is structured correctly from the start. Make sure you receive advice from a tax planning expert – do not rely on a High Street accountant to know all the tweaks that will make a big difference to your long term wealth.

9. **Understand the importance of philanthropy** – Many people only consider this when they have made their fortune, but you will find deep satisfaction in giving even more modest amounts while working to accumulate wealth. You will also bump into people in the charity world that can help in your business and investing life. The bible says that you will be richly rewarded when you give – most are cynical. Until they try it…

10. **You make more money when you sell a business than when you operate it** – develop the mentality of a business investor rather than a business operator and focus on creating a saleable business with a ready made management team that works without you

11. **Grow through acquisition rather than organically** – this will enable you to grow in kangaroo jumps rather than bunny hops as a single deal could double the size of your business in an afternoon. Jonathan runs a whole programme on this at the Dealmakers Academy

12. **Don't retire from something you love!** Friends and family may ask you when you are going to slow down but why should you if you are happy? Retirement is a dangerous concept unless you have a clear idea of what you want to 'retire to'. Most people spend their lives doing things they don't enjoy – if you're lucky enough to find a business or career that is fulfilling keep at is as long as you can!

13. **Turn your Fast Pounds into Slow Pounds** – your salary or income can leave your bank account as quickly as it arrives, so you need to learn to live on 50% of your income and invest the rest in assets such as property that throw off Slow Pounds. Use the slow pounds to pay for the fancy cars and holidays.

14. **Buy the premises you run your business from** – not only does this give you an appreciating asset, it puts you in control of one of your business's biggest overheads – the rent. (I actually own the building my business trades from in my pension plan so my company is paying rent into my pension every month – GR)

15. **Hire employees so you can do the important stuff!** Most business owners try to leave it as long as possible before hiring staff. This is a mistake because you need to think like an Entrepreneur and appoint managers to operate the business. You lead and set the vision, they tidy up the mess and make your vision a reality!

16. **The best opportunities may be overseas** – Frederick discovered Estonia by accident and found enormous opportunity there. The skills and experience he acquired in that young, developing country have helped him think differently to many UK property developers.

17. **Use technology to solve people's problems** – investment involves a lot of paperwork which the Brickowner platform automates. By bringing these costs down the platform is able to allow minimum investments as low as £100 which opens up property investing to a wider audience.

18. **Trust and flexibility are key to customer relationships** – you need to find ways to help people increase their trust in you, for example by offering a low minimum investment to test a new platform, and you need to be flexible so that you fit into people's busy lives in a way that is convenient for them. You just have to look at the growth in online shopping to see how important flexibility and convenience have become.

19. **Do your own due diligence!** Investing in early stage companies is both risky and long term. Make sure you understand what they do, how they make money and how credible their business plan is. Who are their competitors and what differentiates the company you are looking to invest in?

20. **Become a mini Venture Capitalist** – spread your investment across at least 5, preferably 10 companies to increase your chances of at least one being a huge success. A typical VC will expect 3 or 4 companies to fail, 3 or 4 to just about wash their face and 1 or 2 to be successful. Their success should more than cover the cost of the other investments and might just make you a fortune if you discover a unicorn.

21. **Don't Suffer Cobblers Shoes syndrome** – like many entrepreneurs, Luke is totally focussed on his own business and has very few assets outside it. You need to learn that your business exists for one sole purpose – so that you can take money out of it! Read the James Sinclair interview on fast pounds and slow pounds for more on this.

22. **Be Organised!** In your work and your finances. Claer used her organisational skills honed as a secretary to make her a more effective journalist and also to get on top of her personal finances. The most successful people on the planet have the same 24 hours a day as you do – the difference is how effectively you use the time to achieve your goals.

23. **Have a clear mission** – Claer knew early on that she wanted to de-mystify the world of finance for her readers so this helps her choose which topics to write about and how to explain them because she has a clear understanding of the kind of person she is writing for. Note how empathetic she is to the dilemma they face, for example in choosing a cash ISA rather than a stocks and shares product.

24. **Be careful with your money!** Claer's frugal parents ingrained this approach in her childhood which is when our thinking around money is formed. The only way you are certain of becoming wealthy is to form the habit of living within your means, saving and investing regularly. With compounding, even small amounts become millions if you start early enough.

25. **Divorce is the greatest destroyer of wealth** – so choose your life partner carefully and do everything you can to stay together! The dilemma was highlighted by the late Country singer Tammy Wynette whose two greatest hits were 'Stand by your man' and 'D.I.V.O.R.C.E.'

26. **Focus to build wealth, diversify to protect wealth** – not everyone will agree with this one because it's a high risk approach. Choose the right company or sector and you could make a fortune, choose badly and you could set your plan back years. My own approach uses a Wealth Pyramid with different assets at different levels of the pyramid doing a different job for me.

27. **Compounding is the 8th wonder of the world** – nothing new here, but it bears repeating because so few people seem to recognise it and exploit it. Even saving modest sums with average returns can turn into a substantial nest egg if you start young enough. Compounding works on a hockey stick shape so the biggest gains come at the very end. Take a multi-generational view of wealth creation and your family can benefit massively from a plan that covers 30, 40 or 50 years of wealth building.

28. **Invest with your brain, not your gut.** We are not genetically programmed to make good investment decisions. We need to engage our brain and have a clear strategy that we can stick to without panicking if prices move against us.

29. **Financial education needs to be timely.** There's no point in learning about mortgages or utility bills at school because everything will have changed by the time you actually need to choose between suppliers. Even learning about pensions in adulthood is challenging because the politicians keep moving the goal posts.

30. **Be prepared to go against the crowd.** You can't just blindly do the opposite all the time, but there will be occasions when the crowd is wrong and you can make a lot of money with an opposite strategy. Perhaps the biggest example of this is the small group who bet against the US housing market in 2006/2007 as captured in the film and book The Big Short.

31. **Know your numbers** – Nicole used her financial background to model the details of her property projects and managed the budgets day to day to keep everything on track. So many business owners and investors are sloppy when it comes to forecasting, monitoring and managing the key metrics that mean the difference between success and failure.

32. **Cash is king** – linked to point 1, and the most common cause of failure for property investors who grow into property developers. As a rule of thumb Nicole suggests keeping 25% of the overall value of the project in free cash as costs always increase and timescales always lengthen.

33. **Be ready to change your strategy when the market turns** – Nicole was one of the first to see the potential to convert tired HMOs into luxury family homes. When that strategy became crowded she moved to developing and selling flats on a large scale. With the slow sales market she is now pivoting again to a buy and hold rental strategy.

34. **Marketing and sales are vital business skills.** It doesn't matter how great your idea is or how good your product, if you don't know how to market or sell your products and services your business is going to struggle. I remember meeting Dan at several American events where we'd each paid thousands of dollars to learn the latest techniques so we could apply them to our businesses.

35. **Create wealth in business then invest it.** Similar to James Sinclair's approach with fast pounds and slow pounds, Dan uses his businesses to generate rapid profits then takes money off the table into investments like tracker funds and property. Done right, real wealth creation can be 'boring' but predictable, especially when you add in the power of compounding.

36. **Be ready to deal with life's shocks.** His near fatal cycling accident forced Dan to re-think his entire business strategy and set him on the road to the success he enjoys today. Are you the lynchpin of your business? What would happen if you were unable to work for months on end? Take a look at how your business and your investment portfolio is structured and try to create passive income that does not demand your presence.

37. **Treat trading as a business, not a hobby.** If you treat it like a hobby you get hobby results. Treat it like a business by keeping detailed records, logging why you entered trades and what was the outcome. Only by developing this level of discipline and professionalism can you expect to achieve consistent results.

38. **Allow 5-10 years to develop your skills!** Not what you may want to hear, but trading the financial markets is a complex business that needs knowledge, experience and discipline. Remember that 90% of traders lose 90% of their capital in the first 90 days, so if you want to see different results you need to take a different, patient approach.

39. **Don't let the media dictate your strategy.** If anything, treat the mainstream media as a contra-indicator. Much of the negative coverage they specialise in will already be in the price, while markets tend to rise or fall based on a view of future rather than past events. If your market antennae are finely tuned you can go against the crowd and make a killing.

40. **Patience is a virtue!** John waited six years watching an abandoned development on the Ipswich waterfront before making his move to buy it. Even then, he thought he might have blinked too soon. Don't be in a rush, there's always another deal around the corner and it may better than the one you're looking at.

41. **Difficult markets can be more profitable.** If you know what you're doing, and you have the right strategy, you can do things differently from the crowd and make serious money. This is an advanced strategy for experienced developers, so don't try this at home...

42. **Why is the property in the auction?** Ask the estate agent and the auctioneer, then verify the situation with the next door neighbour. There's usually a reason why the property has been put into an auction rather than being sold through a conventional estate agent. Knowing the reason will help you determine whether you've found a bargain or a lemon.

43. **Persistence pays** – look at how hard he had to work to find an opening in journalism before accepting an offer on a local paper in Lincoln – and promptly having to get the map out to see where it was!

44. **Have liquid funds to seize opportunities** – John was offered the chance to part own a race horse for £5,000. That horse went on to win millions in prize money for its owners. John is clearly a spender rather than a saver, and his lack of ready cash forced him to turn down this opportunity. Caveat: We are not suggesting that race horses are a good investment strategy!

45. **Don't be afraid of change** – at several times in his career John did not know what was going to happen next. At the time of our interview he had just walked out on a 25 year career at Radio 5. But he's not worried about the future, he's excited about what might be coming next. Whether you're staring at redundancy or a failing business, stay positive about the new opportunities that life is going to put in front of you.

46. **Follow your dreams** – from his childhood Lego days James wanted to be in the construction industry and went on to achieve great success in multiple senior roles.

47. **Build and maintain a network of contacts** – there's a lot of truth in the cliché that 'it ain't what you know it's who you know'. Relationships are important so work on developing them and don't let them evaporate just because you change roles. Make the effort to stay in touch because you never know when that relationship could come in handy for either of you.

48. **Don't be afraid to re-invent yourself** – just like Docklands has transitioned from run down warehouses to Manhattan on Thames, your career or business can thrive on reincarnation. James has used his appearance on the Apprentice to build a media career alongside his property career. What other talents do you have and how could they be developed to generate new income streams?

49. **Focus on what you can do** – in Aidan's case it took a question from his father to shake him out of depression by ignoring his past failings and focusing on developing his art skills

50. **Invest in your education** – only by learning can you acquire the skills to be successful in your chosen career, business or investing activity. As Jim Rohn said 'formal education will make you a living, self education will make you a fortune'.

51. **Plan your business from the customer's perspective.** Too many entrepreneurs have a good idea then throw time and money at implementing it only to find no one wants to buy it! Far better to find a problem the customer has and help them solve it – like how to invest in art safely and profitably!

About
The Author

Graham Rowan is an internationally renowned speaker, author and television presenter. His mission to end financial illiteracy has taken him to the United Nations in New York, Harvard Business School in Boston and both Houses of Parliament in the UK.

His previous television work includes the series Make Your Money Work and Finding Financial Freedom, as well as documentaries on China's Trillion Dollar Secret and The 3 Steps To Financial Freedom.

An expert investor, Graham helps high net worth individuals and family offices to build and protect their wealth through access to unique alternative investments and sophisticated tax planning strategies.

His previous books are The French Property Secret (2010) and Encounters With Investment Icons (2015).

Graham is married to Daphne and splits his time between homes in Weybridge, Antibes and Montenegro.